A Primer in Stroke Care

Professor A. Magid O. Bakheit, MB (Hons), MD (Glasg),
PhD (Glasg), FRCP (Lond), MSc (Lond), Dip Neurology (lond).

Professor of Neurological Rehabilitation, Universities of Exeter &
Plymouth & Honorary Consultant, Plymouth Primary Care Trust.

authorHOUSE®

AuthorHouse™
1663 Liberty Drive, Suite 200
Bloomington, IN 47403
www.authorhouse.com
Phone: 1-800-839-8640

First published by AuthorHouse 10/3/2007

ISBN: 978-1-4343-1881-7 (sc)

Printed in the United States of America
Bloomington, Indiana

This book is printed on acid-free paper.

PREFACE

Stroke is the commonest neurological disease in adults. It frequently results in serious morbidity and high mortality. It also has a significant impact on those who survive it and on their families, especially on their emotional wellbeing, personal social relationships, and their ability to engage in gainful employment and to pursue leisure activities.

The prognosis for survival and for functional recovery from stroke has improved in recent years in many countries thanks to the better organisation and delivery of the medical and nursing care for these patients, especially in the immediate aftermath of the cerebrovascular event. The use of effective rehabilitation strategies has also improved the patients' chances of reaching their best potential for functional independence. In addition, the routine implementation of strategies for the secondary prevention of stroke has resulted in reduction in stroke recurrence.

Numerous monographs and textbooks about stroke have been published in recent years. However, most of these publications are either too detailed or very specialised and insufficiently comprehensive to be of value as a quick reference for busy clinicians. The aim of this book is to bridge this gap by providing a short, yet comprehensive, and up to date guide to the management of stroke patients. Each chapter concludes with a list of suggested further reading for those who desire more detailed information on a particular subject. It is hoped that doctors, nurses and therapists, as well as medical students, find the text a useful resource.

Professor A.M.O. Bakheit

Plymouth, December 2006

CONTENTS

CHAPTER ONE

THE CLINICO-PATHOLOGICAL SPECTRUM OF STROKE

Definition of stroke
The definition of the World Health Organisation of stroke is now widely adopted and has proved to be useful in clinical practice. According to this definition, a clinical diagnosis of stroke can be made with confidence if the patient presents with a focal neurological deficit that occurs suddenly and lasts more than 24 hours or results in death and the cause of the neurological deficit can only be attributed to a vascular event. When the symptoms resolve in 24 hours or less then the condition is referred to as a transient ischaemic attack (TIA).

Epidemiology
Stroke is the commonest neurological disease worldwide and is a leading cause of death and long-term disability. Community-based studies suggest that the total annual incidence of stroke (i.e. first-ever and recurrent stroke) is between 100 and 290 per 100,000 of the population and is highest in Finland and Japan and lowest in South American countries. Western Europe and North America have an intermediate incidence rate of about 160 cases per 100,000 of the population. The prevalence of stroke in Western Europe is approximately 650 per 100,000 of the population. The variations between countries in the age-adjusted incidence of stroke can be explained by ethnic, environmental and cultural behavioural differences in life style, and by socio-economic factors.

In a given community the incidence and prevalence of stroke are influenced by the ethnic composition of the community, the age and gender structure of the population, and social class. The effect of ethnicity is demonstrated by the higher occurrence of stroke in people of Afro-Caribbean origin compared to that in Caucasians. This difference is present even after adjustment for other stroke risk factors. Afro-Caribbeans also tend to have a higher incidence of hypertensive spontaneous intracerebral haemorrhage and more mortality from stroke than other races. These differences are more pronounced in the younger age groups and tend to become progressively less with advancing age.

The incidence of stroke worldwide increases with increasing age. Epidemiological surveys suggest that after the age of 55 years the risk of having stroke doubles every 10 years. Gender has a similar effect and men tend to have more strokes than women of the same age. A low socio-economic status also correlates with a higher incidence of stroke. Although stroke is primarily a disease of middle and old age, it can also affect children and young adults.

Stroke in childhood and in young adults is relatively rare except in those with haemoglobinopathies. It is a common complication of sickle cell disease (SCD) with a prevalence rate of approximately 4% in populations where SCD is common. The incidence of stroke due to SCD varies with the patient's age. The risk of having a first stroke at the ages of 20, 30 or 45 years has been estimated as 11%, 15% and 24%, respectively. Recurrence of stroke is also common. A history of TIA or meningitis, high systolic blood pressure, raised white cell count and low haemoglobin concentrations are associated with an increased risk of stroke in patients with SCD. Other genetic abnormalities of haemoglobin synthesis also predispose to stroke, but to a lesser degree. For example, the reported prevalence of stroke is 2.4% in subjects who carry both the sickle haemoglobin gene and the β thalassaemia gene (Sβ°).

Stroke risk factors
A stroke risk factor is a condition that predisposes to stroke and also predicts the recurrence of stroke in a person who had a previous cerebrovascular event. Most patients presenting with stroke or TIA have one or more risk factors. However, the relationship between the risk factors and the occurrence of stroke is complex and control of the risk factors does not fully protect against stroke. This is illustrated by a study of the incidence of stroke in Sweden that showed a significant improvement in the control of hypertension and a decrease in cigarette smoking in the adult population between 1971 and 1987 while the incidence of stroke remained unchanged. Nonetheless, assessment for these factors is important for the patient's management in the acute phase of stroke and also for the long-term prevention of stroke recurrence. The main risk factors for stroke and TIA are old age, ethnic origin, hypertension, atrial fibrillation, diabetes mellitus, hyperlipidaemia, cigarette smoking and severe carotid artery stenosis. Frequently, more than one of these factors are present in the same patient.

Age and ethnicity – stroke is predominantly a disease of old age. The incidence of all types of stroke increases progressively from the age of 40 years and peaks in the eighth decade of life.

However, stroke is also relatively common in younger people, with 15-20% of all strokes occuring in people less than 65 years of age. Race is also an important factor. For example, people of Afro-Caribbean, Japanese and Chinese origin have a higher incidence and higher mortality from stroke than any other ethnic groups. Some genetically determined disorders of the blood clotting system, such as protein C deficiency, also predispose to stroke.

Hypertension – is defined as a systolic blood pressure (BP) >140 and diastolic BP >90 mm Hg. Hypertension is by far the commonest and most important risk factor for ischaemic stroke and spontaneous intracerebral haemorrhage. Hypertensive subjects have a twofold increase in the risk of stroke compared to those with a normal BP when other stroke risk factors are controlled for. In addition, one in two patients who present with a first-ever stroke give a history of hypertension or are found to be hypertensive for the first time. There is also a strong correlation between the incidence of stroke and the severity and chronicity of hypertension. Although stroke has been traditionally attributed to systolic and diastolic hypertension, isolated systolic hypertension (defined as systolic BP >160 mm Hg with a normal diastolic) has also recently been recognised as an important risk factor for stroke. Similarly, there appears to be a causal relationship between "white coat" hypertension and cerebrovascular disease, including stroke. (White coat hypertension is abnormally high BP readings in the clinic that are not confirmed on ambulatory measurements. It is presumed to be due to the anxiety associated with attending hospital clinics or being seen by a doctor).

Diabetes mellitus – chronic hyperglycaemia is associated with metabolic disturbances that disrupt the structure and function of small, as well as large blood vessels. The clinical manifestations of the microvascular complications of diabetes are mainly nephropathy, retinopathy and lacunar infarcts. Involvement of large arteries is particularly common in patients with type 2 diabetes. Atheroma may occur in any of the main vascular beds leading to the development of coronary artery disease, peripheral vascular disease and stroke.

The persistent hyperglycaemia, insulin resistance and hyperlipidaemia that are usually seen in patients with type 2 diabetes predispose to, and accelerate the progression of atherosclerosis by altering the function of the vascular endothelium and the structure of the vascular smooth muscle.

These metabolic abnormalities also enhance platelet activity and inhibit fibrinolysis, thus creating favourable conditions for intra-arterial thrombus formation. Therefore, it is not surprising that an estimated 10% of stroke patients have diabetes mellitus and that diabetes increases the risk of stroke by three-fold. The risk of stroke is particularly high among diabetics who are less than 55 years of age. Diabetes also increases the risk of vascular dementia, stroke recurrence and the mortality due to stroke.

Atrial fibrillation (AF) - irrespective of its cause, AF is an independent risk factor for ischaemic stroke. This risk is greatest in those with coexisting heart valve disease. The current evidence suggests that these patients are approximately 20 times more likely to have an arterial thrombo-embolic complication than healthy age- and sex-matched subjects. By contrast, the risk for those with non-valvular AF is increased only fivefold. It is important to recognise that patients with non-valvular AF are not a homogeneous group; some have a higher risk of arterial thrombo-embolism than others. For example, only 0.5% of patients with AF that is not due to organic heart disease have a stroke compared to a 12% incidence rate in those in the high risk group. Predictors of a high risk are hypertension, left ventricular dysfunction, congestive cardiac failure in the preceding three months and a past history of an arterial thrombo-embolism, e.g. TIA or a previous stroke. The co-existance of AF with any of these factors increases the risk of stroke by 7 per cent per year. Other factors that increase the risk of stroke in patients with AF are the presence of thrombi in the left atrial appendage and reduced appendage flow velocities demonstrated on transoesophageal echocardiography. Transcranial Doppler ultrasound monitoring of patients with AF has been suggested as a useful investigation for identifying those with increased risk of stroke, but it does not appear to be reliable.

Hyperlipidaemia - is defined as total serum cholesterol in excess of 5.2 mmol/l, or low density lipoprotein cholesterol (LDL-C) or total fasting triglycerides more than 3 mmol/l and 2.2 mmol/l, respectively. High density lipoprotein cholesterol (HDL-C) confers a protective effect against atherosclerosis. A low HDL-C is, therefore, also an important factor in the aetiopathogenesis of atherosclerosis.

Cigarette smoking - epidemiological studies have shown that cigarette smoking increases the odds of a middle-aged person having a stroke by two to three-fold compared with a nonsmoker. The risk is proportional to the number of cigarettes smoked per day and the length of exposure to smoking. Exposure to environmental tobacco smoke, i.e. passive smoking, has a similar, but probably a less profound, effect. The mechanism by which cigarette smoking causes stroke is not fully understood. However, it is known that cigarette smoking causes dysfunction of the vascular endothelium and increases the stiffness of the blood vessel wall. These are important stages in the development of atherosclerosis. The detrimental effect of smoking on the structure and function of blood vessels appears to be particularly potent in hypertensive and diabetic individuals. Furthermore, smoking is associated with an increase in platelet stickiness, increased fibrinogen levels and blood viscosity. It also lowers high density lipoprotein cholesterol. These abnormalities predispose to intravascular thrombus formation.

Internal carotid artery stenosis – occurs most frequently in the proximal portion of the artery, usually just above the bifurcation of the common carotid artery. Plaque formation is accelerated by the other stroke risk factors. As would be expected, the more risk factors the patient has, the higher the incidence of carotid artery plaques. For example, one study has found that 50% of patients with hypertension, hyperlipidaemia and diabetes mellitus had a carotid artery plaque, compared to an incidence of 20% when the patient had only one of these risk factors.

Atherosclerotic plaques in the carotid arteries lead to their partial or complete occlusion. A ruptured plaque is one of the main sources of cerebral thromboembolism. The degree of risk is proportional to the severity of the stenosis. Patients with >70% internal carotid artery stenosis who present with a stroke or TIA in the carotid artery territory have the highest risk of stroke recurrence. The chance of these patients having another stroke in the following 12 months is 10% with an annual risk of 5% thereafter.

Aetiology of stroke
Stroke may be caused by arterial occlusion resulting from thrombosis or embolism or by rupture of the arterial wall. Vascular occlusion with a thrombus or thrombo-embolism is, by far, the commonest cause of stroke. It accounts for more than 80% of all strokes while spontaneous intracerebral haemorrhage, excluding subarachnoid haemorrhage, is the cause in about 10% of cases. Other causes of stroke include infections of the central nervous system, severe systemic hypotension (especially in the presence

of stenosis of the cerebral arteries), bleeding into a brain tumour and spontaneous dissection of the carotid or vertebral artery.

In-situ thrombosis – thrombus formation in an intracerebral artery is a much less common cause of stroke than thromboembolism. It usually results from hypercoagulable states which may be hereditary or acquired. The best known of the hereditary hypercoagulable (thrombophilic) states are protein S and protein C deficiency. Many acquired conditions, such as malignancy, connective tissue disease, antiphospholipid syndrome, increase the tendency to intravascular thrombosis. Thrombocythaemia and other blood disorders may also predispose to intravascular thrombus formation.

Thromboembolism – atheromatous plaques often form in the proximal portion of the internal carotid arteries and rupture of these plaques frequently results in cerebral thromoembolism and stroke. Occasionally, stroke results from venous (paradoxical) thromboembolism. The source is usually deep vein thrombosis in the lower limbs or pelvis. The thrombus passes to the arterial system through a venous-to-arterial circulation shunt, for example patent foramen ovale.

Embolism - of the intracranial arteries accounts for <15% of all strokes. The commonest source of emboli is vegetations (i.e. deposits of platelets, macrophages, fibrin and micro-organisms) on cardiac valves usually in patients with congenital or rheumatic heart disease and in those with prosthetic heart valves and intra cardiac (mural) thrombi following an acute myocardial infarction. Cardioembolic stroke is frequently associated with atrial fibrillation and congestive heart failure. Other sources of embolism include air embolism during neck and thoracic surgery and fat emboli from fractures of large bones.

Non-traumatic intracerebral haemorrhage - may occur in the subcortical structures and brain stem (deep intracerebral haemorrhage) or in the superficial layers of the cerebral cortex. Deep intracerebral haemorrhage is common in young people and is usually caused by hypertension and/ or rupture of arteriovenous malformations. Occasionally it results from bleeding disorders, eclampsia and the use of illicit drugs that cause a sudden surge in blood pressure (e.g. amphetamines). By contrast, superficial intracerebral haemorrhage often occurs in old people and is frequently recurrent. It is frequently associated with cerebral amyloid angiopathy. The commonest sites of intracerebral haemorrhage are the deep white matter, thalamus, basal ganglia, pons and cerebellum.

Although spontaneous subarachnoid haemorrhage is, by definition, a form of stroke, it has a clinical presentation, course, and prognosis that are different of from those of ischaemic infarction and spontaneous intracerebral haemorrhage. It also requires a different management approach. Subarachnoid haemorrhage is, therefore, considered separately at the end of this section.

Spontaneous arterial dissection - carotid and vertebro-basilar artery dissection is a relatively common cause of stroke in young adults and has been estimated to be the cause of stroke in 20% of those who are less than 45 years of age. The cause of the arterial dissection is not known, but ultrastructural connective tissue abnormalities, usually without other clinical manifestations of a connective tissue disease, have been reported in these patients. Frequently, there is also an increased stiffness of the arterial wall and reduced distensibility of the blood vessel. The dissection is often triggered by minor trauma and leads to haematoma formation in the arterial wall between the intima and adventitia. The clinical features of stroke result from complete vascular occlusion if the intramural haematoma is large or from intravascular thrombosis at the site of the dissection. Propagation of the thrombus or embolisation of distal arteries with thrombus fragments may also occur.

Severe systemic hypotension – irrespective of its aetiology, a transient severe drop in the systemic blood pressure usually causes global cerebral hypoperfusion and may also result in localised or watershed infarcts, i.e. infarcts involving two or more adjacent arterial territories. In these cases the cerebral infarcts usually occur in the presence of partial or complete occlusion of a proximal artery and/ or poor collateral cerebral circulation.

Stroke in the first 6 weeks after myocardial infarction – may result from systemic hypotension due to poor cardiac output or arrhythmia, or an embolism from a thrombus adhering to the cardiac wall (mural thrombus). Patient with a large myocardial infraction and high diastolic blood pressure and atrial fibrillation are more likely to develop this complication.

The classification of stroke
Classification of a disorder into distinct and easily identifiable clinical subgroups is often valuable in helping with the patient's

management plan, including the selection of the appropriate investigations and the optimal treatment strategies. It also frequently provides information on the prognosis of each subgroup of patients with the disorder. Numerous classifications of stroke syndromes have been proposed. One of the most clinically useful classifications is that of the Oxfordshire Community Stroke Project (OCSP) of the 1980s.

The OCSP classification is particularly useful for predicting the prognosis of the common and easily recognisable clinical stroke syndromes. This classification divides the ischaemic stroke syndromes into four main subgroups, namely total anterior circulation infarct (TACI), partial anterior circulation infarct (PACI), posterior circulation infarct (POCI), and lacunar infarcts (LACI). Table 1.1 describes the main clinical features of each syndrome.

Table 1.1
The OCSP classification of ischaemic stroke

Syndrome	Clinical features
TACI	Disorder of higher mental function (e.g. aphasia, apraxia hemispatial neglect, etc) + extensive motor and/ or sensory deficit + hemianopia.
PACI	Any two of the above or only impairment of higher mental function.
LACI	Any of the classical lacunar syndromes (see the relevant section).
POCI	Cerebellar and/ or brain stem symptoms & signs or hemiplegia and contralateral cranial nerve palsy (crossed stroke syndromes).

Patients presenting with TACI have the worst prognosis for survival with an approximately 40% mortality rate in the first month after the stroke onset. The vast majority of those who survive will have a significant long-term functional disability. By contrast, LACI has the best prognosis for both survival and functional independence. Those with PACI and POCI have an intermediate prognosis. This classification also helps with the prediction of recurrence of stroke. The rate of recurrence of stroke in the first year after the index event is highest in patients with POCI. The recurrence rate in these patients is twice that after LACI.

The clinical features of stroke
Stroke may be clinically silent or may result in significant neurological deficits, or even death. The clinical features largely depend on the size and site of the infarct or haemorrhage, the condition of the collateral cerebral circulation and on the restoration of the blood flow in the ischaemic penumbra (see chapter 2).

The condition of the collateral circulation may be affected by the presence of silent stenosis of one or more of the arteries that form the circle of Willis or by the existence of interindividual anatomical variations of the cerebral circulation. For example, occasionally both anterior cerebral arteries arise by one stem from one internal carotid artery. In these situations occlusion of the stem of the anterior cerebral artery invariably results in significant clinical symptoms and signs. By contrast, the clinical features are usually subtle when each anterior cerebral artery arises from the corresponding internal carotid artery because of the collateral flow through the anterior communicating artery.

Although stroke often occurs without prior warning, some patients report prodromal symptoms. For example, a single or multiple TIAs may precede the onset of an ischaemic stroke by days or weeks. Patients presenting with spontaneous carotid or vertebro-basilar artery dissection usually give a history of minor neck trauma and complain of headaches for days before they develop the typical neurological signs which are often progressive.

Frequently stroke patients complain of non-specific symptoms that cannot be directly related to the primary neurological deficit. These symptoms include excessive fatigue, poor mental concentration and sleep disturbances. Abdominal discomfort and dyspepsia due to (neurogenic) gastric erosions are sometimes reported de novo following intracerebral haemorrhage.

Fatigue is common after stroke and has been reported in up to 75% of patients. However, it is not clear whether it is a primary feature of stroke or is due to depression. (Depression is common complication of stroke, see chapter 4). Other possible reasons for fatigue following stroke include sleep disturbances and the adverse effects of some of the commonly used drugs, such as beta-blockers and antihypertensive medication. Stroke patients usually complain of severe exhaustion and aversion to physical and mental activity. There are no specific features of post-stroke fatigue that distinguish them from those due to depression. However, apathy, loss of interest, anhedonia and the preponderance of "biological features" such as weight loss, poor or excessive appetite and insomnia, are thought to favour the diagnosis of depression.

The sleep disturbances that are commonly associated with stroke are insomnia, hypersomnolence and reversed sleep pattern. Insomnia after stroke is usually caused by environmental factors, such as noise or light, and/ or emotional and psychological factors. On the other hand, excessive sleep is often due to fatigue and lack of stimulation, but in some cases it is a direct result of the neurological deficit. Typically, severe and persistent hypersomnolence is associated with thalamic and brain stem stroke.

In the early period after stroke most patients also develop disorders of breathing during sleep and nocturnal hypoxia which is often severe despite normal oxygen saturations during the day. The hypoxia may be either due to impaired central regulation of respiration (leading to central sleep apnoea) or due to sleep-related narrowing or obstruction of the upper airways. Weakness of the diaphragm and intercostal muscles and chronic respiratory failure may also occur. Intercurrent respiratory tract infections, pulmonary embolism and overt or silent pulmonary aspiration due to dysphagia may aggravate the hypoxia. Sleep apnoea (central or obstructive) is common after stroke, especially in those with hypertension and obesity. It is characterised by frequent, long periods (>10 seconds) of cessation of breathing, excessive snoring and daytime sleepiness.

The general physical examination of a stroke patient may reveal evidence of peripheral vascular disease or stroke risk factors.

For example, the finding of a carotid bruit is a valuable clue to the presence of carotid artery stenosis, although there is no consistent relationship between the two.

The main stroke syndromes
There is a good correlation between the clinical features of stroke and the vascular territory involved. This correlation is not absolute because some degree of overlap between the vascular territories is usually present and also because interindividual variations in the vascular anatomy occasionally occur. Nonetheless, a sound knowledge of the brain regional blood supply is important for the accurate diagnosis of stroke and for the patient's management. It is also useful for predicting the prognosis for survival and for functional recovery.

As mentioned earlier, from a clinical point of view it is useful to consider the vascular supply to the brain in terms of anterior and posterior circulation. The anterior circulation arises from the internal carotid artery which divides into anterior cerebral, middle cerebral, posterior communicating, ophthalmic and choroidal arteries. The arteries that make the posterior circulation are branches of the vertebro-basilar system and include the posterior cerebral (sometimes arises from the internal carotid artery), the anterior inferior cerebellar, posterior inferior cerebellar and the paramedian medullary and pontine arteries. Each of these arteries supplies specific brain structures (see table 1.2).

Table 1.2
The regional blood supply of the brain

Artery	Structures supplied
Middle cerebral	*Cortical branches* - sensory & motor cortex (except leg area), language & auditory areas. *Deep branches* - basal ganglia, internal & external capsule.
Anterior cerebral	*Cortical branches* - corpus callosum, medial aspect of hemisphere, upper part of the precentral gyrus (the leg motor area). *Deep branches* – anterior limb of internal capsule, head of caudate nucleus.
Posterior communicating	Medial thalamus.
Choroidal	Globus pallidus, internal capsule (posterior limb), optic tract & radiation, limbic system, choroidal plexus.
Posterior cerebral	*Cortical branches* - occipital & medial temporal lobes. *Deep branches* - thalamus, basal ganglia, brain stem (interpeduncular region).
Posterior inferior cerebellar	Cerebellar hemisphere & vermis, dorso-lateral part of medulla oblongata
Anterior inferior & superior cerebellar	Most of cerebellum.

Internal carotid artery (ICA)

ICA stenosis or complete occlusion may be clinically silent. However, when it is symptomatic it results in the syndrome of total anterior circulation stroke (see table 1.1). Amaurosis fugax, i.e. transient monocular blindness, frequently precedes the occlusion of the ICA and results from thromboembolism of the ophthalmic or retinal artery.

Middle cerebral artery (MCA)

The MCA divides into cortical and lenticulo-striate (deep) branches. The cortical portion of the MCA consists of two major divisions: superior and inferior. These divide further into orbital, frontal, parietal and temporal branches and supply the sensory and motor cortex (except the leg area which receives blood supply from the anterior cerebral artery), and the language and auditory areas. The lenticulo-striate branches, which arise from the proximal portion of the MCA, supply the basal ganglia, internal capsule and the periventricular part of the corona radiata.

Stroke involving the superior division of the MCA typically results in hemiplegia (the arm is more severely affected than the leg), hemisensory loss and hemianopia. In addition, limb and bucco-facial (oral) apraxia and aphasia are present with dominant hemisphere lesions and hemispatial neglect and constructional apraxia with non-dominant hemisphere stroke. Occlusion of the inferior division of the left MCA usually causes only Wernicke aphasia. Other symptoms are frequently absent or only mild and transient.

Occlusion of the lenticul-striate arteries is usually due to emboli from the heart or from an atheromatous plaque in the cervical portion of the internal carotid artery. A cardiac source of emboli should be suspected if there is haemorrhagic transformation of the infarct and is relatively common in children and young adults. Lenticulo-striate stroke results in hemiplegia, hemianopia and sensory symptoms. Mild dysphasia and unilateral hemispatial neglect may be present possibly because of the importance of the basal ganglia in language processing, the loss of function in the ischaemic penumbra or the effects of diaschisis. (Diaschisis a phenomenon characterised by impairment of function in a brain region distant from, but functionally and anatomically related to, the site of the primary lesion).

Anterior cerebral artery (ACA)

Stroke in the ACA territory is rare (<2% of all strokes) and usually results from a thromboembolism from the internal carotid artery or from a cardiac embolism. ACA stroke causes crural monoplegia or hemiparesis that predominantly affects the leg, transient akinetic mutism and mood disturbances. In addition, transcortical aphasia or hemispatial neglect may be present depending on whether the dominant or non-dominant hemisphere is involved.

Posterior cerebral artery (PCA)

Like the MCA, the PCA has cortical and deep branches. The cortical branches supply the occipital cortex and the medial structures of the temporal lobe. A stroke in this vascular territory causes a visual field defect (usually upper quadrantanopia) and a wide range of visual symptoms, including visual hallucinations in the blind fields, visual colour agnosia, object agnosia, prosopagnosia (inability to recognise familiar faces), and other visual perceptual difficulties. Rarely, patients may develop the syndrome of alexia without agraphia. These patients are not able to read, but they can write and have normal language function.

The deep branches of the PCA perfuse the thalamus and the interpeduncular region of the upper brain stem. Their occlusion or rupture results in a thalamic stroke (see below) or Weber syndrome which consists of ipsilateral third nerve palsy and a contralateral hemiplegia. Bilateral occlusion of the PCA (or occlusion of the upper part of the basilar artery) leads to cortical blindness.

Thalamic stroke

The thalamus is one of the commonest sites of stroke. About 25% of all cases of spontaneous intracerebral haemorrhage occur in the thalamus. It has also been estimated that isolated thalamic infarcts account for more than 10% of the posterior circulation ischaemic strokes. Thalamic stroke is frequently caused by hypertension which is found in 75% of cases. Rarely, cardiac emboli result in thalamic infarcts.

The thalamus is a complex structure with many diverse functions. The sensory fibres which form the medial and lateral laminiscus converge in the thalamic nuclei (third order sensory neurones) before they ascend to the sensory cortex. Thalamic nuclei also contribute to a range of cognitive functions, including alertness, motivation, mood, memory, emotional responses and language

19

processing. Consequently, thalamic stroke results in a variety of different combinations of sensori-motor, neuropsychological and behavioural symptoms.

The clinical features of thalamic infarction can be grouped into four major syndromes depending on the part of the thalamus that has been affected. However, it should be emphasised that there is often a considerable overlap in the clinical presentation because of the frequent interindividuals anatomical variations in the blood supply of the thalamus. Thalamic haemorrhage is also rarely confined to one group of nuclei. The main thalamic stroke syndromes are:

The syndrome of the tuberothalamic artery (also known as the polar artery and the anterior thalamo-perforating artery) occlusion – causes reduced arousal and motivation, impairment of memory and learning, blunted emotional responses, dysphasia and personality change.

The syndrome of the paramedian artery *(posterior thalamo-perforating artery) occlusion* – unilateral lesions result mainly in disorders of arousal and memory. Rarely, the left and right paramedian arteries arise from a common stem and embolism of this artery causes bilateral paramedian thalamic infarcts. Patients with the bilateral paramedian thalamic syndrome typically present with transient coma or fluctuating level of consciousness. They then develop symptoms of akinetic mutism, severe amnesia, confabulation, verbal perseveration, poor insight, vertical gaze palsy and unilateral hemispatial neglect.

The syndrome of the inferolateral (thalamo-geniculate) artery occlusion - most patients with infarcts in this arterial territory develop hemianaesthesia, motor weakness, mild dysphasia and hemispatial neglect. However, occasionally the clinical presentation is dominated by features of the Dejerine-Roussy syndrome.

Dejerine-Roussy syndrome is an uncommon consequence of thalamic stroke. Its clinical picture consists mainly of severe persistent pain that is resistant to analgesic drugs. The pain may occur spontaneously or may be triggered by touching the skin. In addition to the characteristic pain, the patient often complains of other sensory symptoms, e.g. dysaesthesia and hyperaesthesia. Mild hemiparesis, choreoathetoid movements of the paretic limbs and mild hemiataxia are also usually present.

The syndrome of the posterior choroidal artery occlusion – the main features of this syndrome are visual field deficits, hemianaesthesia, hemiparesis and dystonia. Transcortical aphasia may also be present.

Stroke involving the caudate nucleus
Stroke restricted to the caudate nucleus is relatively rare. It results in disturbances of behaviour, involuntary movements, dysarthria and dysphonia. The behavioural abnormalities usually consist of apathy and diminished spontaneous motor activity and speech. However, in some patients psycho-motor agitation is a prominent symptom. Unilateral hemispatial neglect or dysphasia (depending on whether the right or left side is affected) may also be present. Most patients with caudate infarcts also have hemiplegia because of the proximity of the lesion to the internal capsule.

The lateral medullary syndrome
The lateral medullary (Wallenberg) syndrome may result from occlusion of the lateral branch of the posterior inferior cerebellar artery (PICA), the vertebral artery, or any of the three lateral medullary arteries. The complete clinical syndrome is due to damage to the inferior surface of the cerebellum, the sensory and sympathetic fibres in the pons, the vestibular nuclei, and the nuclei of the V, IX, and X cranial nerves.

The clinical presentation is usually with headaches, vertigo and vomiting of sudden onset. Patients may also complain of a hoarse voice and difficulties with swallowing. The main findings on neurological examination consist of weakness of the soft palate, an absent gag reflex and a combination of cerebellar and lower cranial nerve signs and Horner's syndrome (ptosis, enophthalmos, miosis and reduced sweating). The sensory signs are typical. Involvement of the trigeminal nerve nucleus leads to sensory loss in the face ipsilateral to the lesion and interruption of the pontine sensory pathways causes hemisensory loss in the limbs on the contralateral side.

The locked in stroke syndrome
This is a rare, and usually fatal stroke syndrome. It results from occlusion of the basilar artery. Those who survive are left with severe disability. The clinical presentation consists of paralysis of all skeletal muscles except the extra ocular and eyelid muscles. In addition, the patients develop anarthria and dysphagia.

Cognitive function, including language, is intact unless the patient has generalised cerebrovascular disease or other coincidental disorder of the cerebral cortex. The rhythm of sleep-wake cycles is not affected and the patients have awareness of self and of their environment. Language comprehension and awareness of self and of the surrounding environment distinguish the locked in syndrome from the persistent vegetative state.

Lacunar infarcts
Lacunes are deep, small (<15 mm) cavities in the brain tissue. They are usually caused by occlusion of a single perforating artery due to lipohyalinosis – a degenerative disorder of small arteries. They may also result from in situ formation of an atherosclerotic plaque or microembolism. Lacunar infarcts frequently occur in the internal capsule, corona radiata, thalamus and pons. They are due to small vessel disease and the carotid and vertebro-basilar arteries are not affected except in cases of coincidental atheroma.

Most studies suggest that lacunar infarcts account for 6-12% of all hospitalised stroke patients. By contrast, community studies have reported that approximately a quarter of strokes are due to lacunar infarcts. Lacunar stroke is usually associated with cigarette smoking, longstanding hypertension and diabetes mellitus. In about 80% of cases the infarcts are clinically silent. However, multiple lacunar infarcts of the basal ganglia, the frontal lobes and periventricular white matter often lead to cognitive impairment culminating in the development of vascular dementia and "vascular" parkinsonism.

Sometimes lacunar infarcts produce well-defined clinical symptoms and signs and are known as the classical lacunar syndromes (CLS). Table 1.3 gives a brief description of the five CLS and the site of small vessel occlusion in each of them. Typically, the CLS occur on awakening from sleep and they are rarely preceded by TIAs. The classical lacunar syndromes do not cause cognitive impairment or other deficits of higher mental function.

Table 1.3 - The classical lacunar syndromes

Lacunar syndrome	Clinical features	Site of lesion
Pure motor hemi-plegia	Isolated hemiplegia. Transient sensory symptoms may occur. Accounts for >50% of CLS.	Internal capsule, basis pontis
Dysarthria-clumsy hand syndrome	Dysarthria, clumsiness of hand, mild hemiparesis, impaired balance. No sensory symptoms.	Basis pontis
Ataxic hemiparesis	Hemiparesis, cerebellar ataxia, no dysarthria, sensory symptoms frequent.	Pons, internal capsule
Pure sensory stroke	Hemianaesthesia only.	Thalamus, internal capsule
Sensorimotor stroke	Hemiplegia and hemisensory loss. Cognition, language, praxis and visual function are intact.	Thalamus, internal capsule

Differential diagnosis of stroke

Although a number of neurological disorders can resemble stroke, an incorrect diagnosis is usually made in only a small minority of cases if the WHO diagnostic criteria of stroke are used. Nonetheless, certain conditions may be confused with stroke. These include epileptic seizures, migraine, acute and chronic subdural haematoma, brain tumours, hypoglycaemic episodes and the "functional decompensation" of a previous stroke.

Patients with epilepsy occasionally develop transient hemiparesis or hemiplegia (Todd's paralysis) and/ or aphasia after an epileptic seizure. These symptoms can easily be confused with stroke, especially as epileptic seizures may occur de novo at the onset of a cerebrovascular event. The cause of post-epileptic aphasia and Todd's paralysis is not known, but is thought to be secondary to focal metabolic changes triggered by the epileptic discharge and leading to "neuronal exhaustion". An alternative view is that they result from excessive neuronal inhibition.

There are no reliable clinical features that differentiate Todd's paralysis from hemiplegic stroke. The severity of Todd's paralysis is variable and ranges from mild weakness to complete hemiplegia. The weakness usually resolves after several hours, but may persist for a few days. A history of epilepsy is helpful in the diagnosis and it is important to emphasise that Todd's paralysis can occur for the first time several years after the onset of epilepsy. CT angiography or diffusion-weighted MRI head scans are the most reliable methods of distinguishing Todd's paralysis from hemiplegia due to stroke.

There is a complex causal relationship between migraine and stroke. Severe, frequent migraine (especially with aura) is a risk factor for ischaemic stroke and for recurrence of stroke in young women, even in the absence of other risk factors. The risk appears to be higher in those who also have a family history of migraine and it progressively decreases after the age of 45 years. Migraine is also associated with a higher incidence of spontaneous carotid and vertebro-basilar artery dissection.

Frequently, it is difficult to make a confident diagnosis of migraine-induced stroke because young subjects with a history of migraine are also liable to have a stroke from other causes. In addition, migraine may be a symptom of a neurological disorder that also causes stroke (e.g. cerebral autosomal dominant angiopathy with subcortical infarcts and leukoencephalopathy – CADASIL). Nonetheless, the diagnostic accuracy of migraine-induced stroke is improved if the following conditions are satisfied: the infarct causing the neurological deficit should be demonstrable on brain imaging and its site must correspond to the migraine aura. In addition, the stroke must occur during the migraine attack and other causes of stroke must be excluded.

Severe hypoglycaemia is a rare cause of hemiplegia and, less often, other focal neurological signs. Hypoglycaemic hemiplegia may be confused with TIAs or stroke. The mechanism by which neuroglycopenia results in focal neurological damage is not clear. However, the deficit is usually completely reversible if the hypoglycaemia is corrected promptly. Consequently, hypoglycaemia should be excluded, as soon as possible, in all patients on insulin or oral hypoglycaemic drugs who present with a possible diagnosis of stroke.

Acute (≤72 hours old), subacute and chronic (> 20 days old) subdural haematoma can be confused with stroke. Patients may present with headaches and mental confusion or with focal neurological signs, including hemiplegia, aphasia or gait ataxia. A history of head trauma, treatment with anticoagulants and alcohol abuse is often present. In rare occasions, the clinical presentation of brain tumours is similar to that of stroke, especially if infarct or haemorrhage occurs in the tumour mass. Brain imaging is required for confirmation of the diagnosis of subdural haematomas and tumours and a CT scan is sufficient in most cases.

Rarely, an acute illness in a person with a chronic neurological disability, e.g. due to a previous stroke, leads to increase in the existing neurological deficits and deterioration in motor or cognitive function. For example, deterioration in the mobility of a previously ambulant stroke patient and increase in the muscle weakness or spasticity are sometimes the only clinical manifestations of a urinary tract infection, dehydration or electrolyte imbalance. Intercurrent illness may also cause deterioration in other functions, including increase in the severity of pre-existing dysphagia, dysphasia, dysarthria or cognitive impairment. This functional decompensation and the associated change in the neurological deficit may be confused with extension of a recent stroke or stroke recurrence. In these circumstances, the diagnostic work up should include screening for coincidental acute illness with the appropriate laboratory tests and radiological investigations.

An important aspect of stroke management is to distinguish spontaneous intracerebral haemorrhage from ischaemic stroke. An onset following physical exertion, severe headache and vomiting preceding the stroke and rapid deterioration in the level of consciousness are thought to be characteristic of stroke due to intracerebral haemorrhage. However, these symptoms do not reliably differentiate between ischaemic and haemorrhagic stroke and brain imaging is necessary for making an accurate diagnosis.

Diagnostic investigations

The diagnostic investigations of a patient presenting with a possible stroke should include brain imaging to confirm the diagnosis and type of stroke (i.e. haemorrhagic or ischaemic) and tests to screen for stroke risk factors. In addition, a baseline measurement of the renal and hepatic function and blood clotting is usually necessary to help with the selection of the dose and type of medication in patients who require drug treatment.

Brain imaging – a computerised tomographic (CT) head scan without contrast enhancement is the first choice radiological investigation of stroke. It frequently confirms the diagnosis and it is more widely available and has a lower cost compared to other forms of brain imaging, such as magnetic resonance imaging (MRI) scans. However, CT is much less sensitive than MRI, especially for brain stem, cerebellar and small lesions and for the detection of minor degrees of haemorrhagic transformation of infarcts. Furthermore, a CT scan does not reliably distinguish between ischaemia and haemorrhage after the first two weeks of stroke. However, it can demonstrate clearly whether the stroke involves a single area or more than one vascular territory, e.g. as in the case of watershed infarcts. CT scans also provide useful prognostic information, especially when the radiological data are considered in conjunction with the clinical findings. The use of CT contrast enhancement is not recommended in cases of suspected acute cerebral infarction, as it may lead to haemorrhagic transformation of the infarct. (Haemorrhagic transformation occurs due to leakage of red blood cells from blood vessels adjacent to the infarct as a result of disruption of the blood brain barrier).

As shown in figure 1.1, the typical CT appearance of an acute cerebral infarct is a low attenuation area corresponding to a vascular territory with or without a mass effect, such as shift of brain mid line structures, due to cerebral oedema. (Attenuation is the X-ray absorption value for a slice of brain tissue). In some cases the infarct is isodense, i.e. has an attenuation value which is similar to that of the healthy brain tissue. In these cases the CT scan appears normal, although subtle changes, e.g. sulcal effacement, are often present. Isodense lesions usually evolve into the typical radiological appearance of an infarct within a few hours of an ischaemic stroke. CT scans may also show areas of patchy high attenuation within the low attenuation area. This suggests haemorragic transformation of the infarct. An infarct matures after a month or so of the stroke onset and this is confirmed by the loss of tissue in the area of low attenuation on the CT scan.

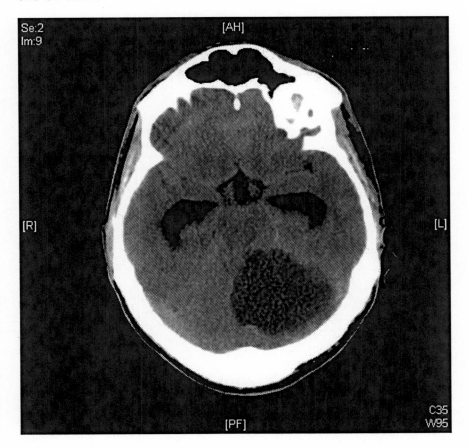

Early confirmation of the ischaemic aetiology of stroke is essential when thrombolysis is being considered. However, this is not always possible with conventional CT or T2–weighted MRI brain scans. In the first 3-6 hours after stroke an ischaemic infarct is visible in only 30-60% of cases with these investigations. Furthermore, the infarct size (which is an important factor in the consideration for thrombolysis) cannot be reliably determined until after the first 12 hours. The investigation of choice for the early diagnosis of cerebral infarction is a diffusion-weighted MRI scan. It has a detection rate of 98%.

In contrast to infarcts, intracerebral haemorrhage results in high attenuation lesions (see figure 1.2). Sometimes a narrow ring of low attenuation area surrounding the hyperdense lesion is also seen. Oedema of the surrounding tissue and/ or extension of the bleed into the cerebral ventricles or subarachnoid space may be present. The high attenuation changes to low attenuation after two or three weeks of the brain haemorrhage and then it is impossible to distinguish a haemorrhage from an infarct on CT scans. Occasionally, the CT scan is helpful in demonstrating the presence of an underlying lesion, e.g. an arterio-venous malformation, as the cause of the bleeding. However, in these cases further imaging with MRI head scans and/ or cerebral angiography is usually required.

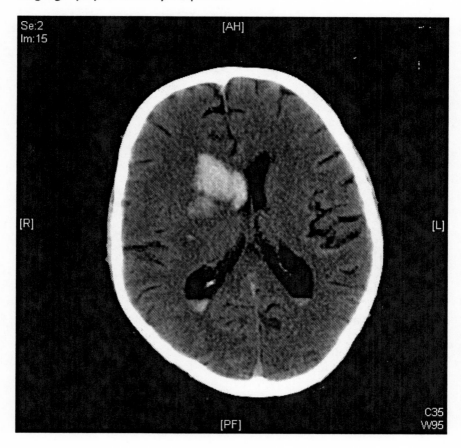

Spontaneous dissection of the carotid and vertebral arteries is a relatively common cause of stroke in young people. Although selective angiography is the gold standard investigation for the diagnosis of arterial dissection, this investigation is seldom necessary. Non-invasive investigations, such as colour duplex ultrasonography, MRI scans and magnetic resonance angiography (MRA) are usually adequate for confirmation of the diagnosis.

Duplex ultrasonography is reliable and sensitive, especially for the diagnosis of carotid artery dissection. It confirms the typical haemodynamic changes of arterial narrowing and also demonstrates characteristic echographic patterns, e.g. localised dilatation of the artery, a true and false lumen, echosignal of the mural haematoma, tapering of the arterial lumen and the absence of an atheromatous plaque.

MRI scans detect carotid artery dissection in about 80% of cases. They are less sensitive for detecting vertebral artery dissection. Partial arterial occlusion results in a high attenuation signal (because of the intravascular haematoma) and an adjacent area of low attenuation. The latter sign is due to blood flow in the narrowed lumen of the artery. It is absent when the occlusion is complete. The diagnostic sensitivity and specificity of MRA exceed that of MRI scans and ultrasonography.

Screening for stroke risk factors – the diagnostic work up of stroke should routinely include screening for the main modifiable stroke risk factors. Blood glucose and serum cholesterol should be checked and in diabetics the quality of glycaemic control should be established (by measuring the level of glycated haemoglobin – HbA1c). An ECG will provide a record of cardiac rhythm. It is also essential to exclude significant internal carotid artery stenosis with an ultrasound Doppler study in all patients presenting with an ischaemic anterior circulation stroke who have no contra indications to surgery. Additional investigations are sometimes required when less common causes of stroke are suspected. Examples are given in table 1.4.

Table 1.4

Suspected cause of stroke	Recommended investigation
Embolism (cardiac source)	Transthoracic/ transoesophageal echocardiography
Protein S or C deficiency	Thrombophilia screen
Antiphospholipid syndrome	Lupus anticoagulants
Neurosyphilis	Syphilis serology
Sickle cell disease	Sickling test, haemoglobin electrophoresis
Bleeding disorders	Blood clotting studies
Temporal arteritis	Temporal artery biopsy

Prognosis of stroke
The prognosis of stroke may be viewed in terms of the chances of surviving the acute cerebrovascular event, stroke recurrence and also the prognosis for functional recovery. All of these are influenced by the size and site of the stroke and the previous health of the patient. The quality of the medical and nursing care for stroke patients is also important and may account for the reported significant differences in the mortality rate and the level of long-term dependency of these patients.

The size and site of stroke have an important effect on prognosis. For example, total anterior circulation stroke carries the worst prognosis for survival and for functional recovery. Approximately 40% of these patients die in the first month after stroke and the death rate increases to 60% by the end of the first year. Similarly, more than a third of those who survive will remain severely disabled and functionally dependent one year later. By contrast, the death rate following lacunar infarcts is less than 3% in the first month and is about 10% in the first year after stroke. Partial anterior circulation and posterior circulation infarcts have an intermediate mortality rate.

Early and late survival -
Stroke is a major cause of death and disability throughout the world. Mortality from stroke in Western Europe has declined in the last three or four decades. This is probably due to a combination of better medical and nursing care in the acute stage, and reduced disease severity. Nonetheless, stroke remains a leading cause of death and long-term functional disability. Between 20-30% of patients who are admitted to hospital with an acute ischaemic stroke die in the first four weeks. (The overall death rate in the first month after stroke in community samples is 10%). The mortality rate after spontaneous intracerebral haemorrhage is even higher.

Early death after stroke is usually due to cardiac arrhythmias, massive pulmonary embolism, pneumonia or brain stem compression due to extensive cerebral oedema. The main predictors of a high mortality after stroke are: onset with coma or a combination of impaired consciousness, dense hemiplegia and failure of conjugate eye movements towards the side of the limb weakness. Urinary incontinence is also a poor prognostic sign for survival. Interestingly, urinary incontinence appears to be a more sensitive predictor than reduced level of consciousness.

The prognosis of spontaneous intracerebral haemorrhage is usually worse than that of cerebral infarction and generally correlates with the size of the haematoma and its effects on brain function. For example, patients with a large thalamic haemorrhage (haematoma > 2 cm in diameter or 4 ml in volume), have a 25% early mortality rate, if they present with impaired level of consciousness or extension of the bleed into the ventricles. The development of hydrocephalus in the first week and radiological evidence of displacement of midline brain structures are also poor prognostic signs.

Recurrence rate of stroke –
The risk of stroke recurrence in the first 30 days after the cerebrovascular event is highest in patients with severe diabetes, congestive heart failure or a history of a previous stroke. Major stroke has an annual recurrence rate of 9%. By contrast, 6% of patients with a minor stroke would be expected to have another one within a year. The prognosis of the classical lacunar syndromes is generally good. Recurrence in the first month is rare but one in five patients will have another lacunar infarct within a year and this usually occurs in a brain region different from that of the index stroke. The highest recurrence rate is associated with posterior circulation infarcts. It is approximately 25% in the first month and 20% in the first year.

Functional recovery -
About 80% of those who survive the acute cerebrovascular event regain some degree of independence with mobility and activities of daily living and most of the functional improvement is usually achieved in about three months from the stroke onset. However, there is a subgroup of patients, e.g. those with severe and persistent hemispatial neglect, in whom functional recovery is more slow and is often delayed. A number of demographic and clinical variables appear to influence the rate and extent of recovery. Urinary incontinence in the first seven days after stroke has been consistently shown to carry a poor prognosis for functional independence at six months. Other predictors of poor functional recovery are old age, a severe initial motor deficit, poor sitting balance at 2-3 weeks, cognitive impairment, persistent apraxia, severe hemispatial neglect and Wernicke aphasia.

The type of stroke is also important. Functional recovery from lacunar stroke is usually complete in about 6-8 weeks except in lesions involving the basal ganglia. By contrast, after total anterior circulation stroke functional recovery is relatively rare and, when it occurs, it is usually limited. In one study, three quarters of patients with internal carotid artery occlusion were either dead or severely disabled after a mean follow up period of 15 months.

At present about 20% of stroke survivors in Britain are admitted to institutional care. This is largely because of their poor recovery from stroke and the very high degree of functional dependency, although socio-economic factors, such as the availability of informal social support, are also important.

Transient ischaemic attacks
Like ischaemic stroke, a transient ischaemic attack (TIA) is a focal neurological deficit due to arterial occlusion, but the symptoms and signs are transient and last no longer than 24 hours. TIAs result from embolism, usually with platelets/fibrin material from an atherosclerotic plaque in the proximal segment of the internal carotid or vertebral arteries. Other sources of emboli include a mural cardiac thrombus, vegetations from cardiac valves and fragments of cardiac tumours, such as left arterial myxomas. Occasionally, the embolus is an air bubble entering the arterial circulation during neck or thoracic surgery. It is not possible to confidently establish the source of the embolus from the clinical symptoms and signs alone, although it is generally thought that recurrent TIAs that are clinically similar indicate the presence of an atheromatous plaque in a proximal artery. This contrasts with recurrent TIAs due to cardiac emboli which often produce a different clinical pattern each time.

The clinical features of a TIA depend on the affected vascular territory. For example, embolism of the choroidal or ophthalmic arteries leads to transient monocular blindness (amaurosis fugax), whereas a TIA involving a branch of the middle cerebral artery may cause a hemiplegia, hemisensory loss or a visual field defect.

A patient with a TIA is likely to develop a stroke in the future. The annual risk of stroke is 3.7% for TIAs in the cerebral hemispheres, brain stem or cerebellum, but is lower (2.2%) for patients presenting with amaurosis fugax. Consequently, all patients with TIAs should be routinely screened for stroke risk factors and any identified modifiable risk factors should be corrected.

Spontaneous subarachnoid haemorrhage
Non-traumatic subarachnoid haemorrhage (SAH) is a relatively common cause of stroke. It is usually due to rupture of saccular (berry) aneurysms and is frequently associated with hypertension. Saccuar aneurysms are thought to result from developmental or acquired defects in the structure of the vascular wall and usually occur at the site of the bifurcation of the main cerebral arteries, most frequently the anterior and posterior communicating and the middle cerebral arteries. The weakness of the arterial wall causes the intima to bulge outward. The aneurismal sac gradually enlarges and may rupture causing leakage of blood into the subarachnoid space and sometimes also into the brain tissue and ventricles. Typically, berry aneurysms are 10 millimetres

33

in diameter, but they can enlarge to 3 or more centimetres in diameter. In some cases of SAH an aneurysm is not seen on four vessel angiography and this "idiopathic" form usually results in mild symptoms and has a benign prognosis. Rarely, the aneurysms are due to septic arterial embolisation, e.g. in patients with subacute bacterial endocarditis, and are known as mycotic aneurysms.

Hypertension and cigarette smoking are the main risk factors for SAH. The peak incidence of aneurysmal subarachnoid haemorrhage is the fourth to the sixth decade of life. The clinical presentation is typically with severe "thunderclap" headache, vomiting, photophobia and neck stiffness with or without loss or impairment of consciousness. Epileptic seizures are common. Clinical examination confirms the presence of Kernig's sign of meningeal irritation (an attempt by the examiner to extend the patient's knee from a position of 90 degrees flexion at the hip causes severe back and neck pain). Focal neurological signs, such as third nerve palsy or hemiplegia, may be present from the outset or develop a few days later usually due to secondary vascular spasm. Severe cognitive deficits and behavioural difficulties are common in all, but the mildest of cases.

CT head scans demonstrate the leakage of blood in the subarachnoid space in most cases. Examination of the cerebrospinal fluid for red blood cells and xanthochromia is indicated when the CT scan appearances are normal, but cerebral angiography is needed for a definitive diagnosis and for the accurate identification of the ruptured aneurysm. Management of acute subarachnoid haemorrhage consists of life support and symptomatic treatment. Administration of Nimodipine improves the neurological outcomes by preventing prolonged vasospasm. Surgical clipping or coil embolisation of the aneurysm is indicated in all but those with a very poor prognosis because of the high recurrence rate of fatal haemorrhage (20% in the first 2 weeks after the index bleed and 50% at 6 months after the index bleed).

RECOMMENDED FURTHER READING

Aho K, Harmsen P, Hatano S, et al. Cerebrovascular disease in the community: results of a WHO collaborative study. *Bull WHO* 1980; **58**: 113-130

Asherson RA, Khamashta MA, Ordi-Ros J, et al. The "primary" antiphospholipid antibody syndrome: major clinical and serological features. *Medicine* 1989; **68**: 336-374

Bamford J, Sandercock P, Dennis M, Burn J, Warlow C. Classification and natural history of clinically identifiable subtypes of cerebral infarction. *Lancet* 1991; **337**: 1521-1526

Bogousslavsky J, Regli F, Uske A. Thalamic infarcts: clinical syndromes, etiology and prognosis. *Neurology* 1988; **38**: 837-848

Chamorro A, Sacco R L, Mohr J P, et al. Clinical-computed tomographic correlations of lacunar infarction in the Stroke Data Bank. *Stroke* 1991; **22**: 175-181

Dejerine J, Roussy G. The thalamic syndrome. *Arch Neurol* 1969; **20**: 560-562

Kumral E, Kocaer T, Ertubey NO, Kumral K. Thalamic haemorrhage. A prospective study of 100 patients. *Stroke* 1995; **26**: 964-970

Kwakkel G, Wagenaar RC, Kollen BJ, Lankhorst GJ. Predicting disability in stroke – a critical review of the literature. *Age Aging* 1996; **25**: 479-489

Schmahmann JD. Vascular syndromes of the thalamus. *Stroke* 2003; **34**: 2264-2278

Stegmayer B, Asplund K, Wester PO. Trends in incidence, case fatality rate and severity of stroke in Northern Sweden, 1985-1991. *Stroke* 1994; **25**: 1738-1745

Tuszynski MH, Petito CK, Levy DE. Risk factors and clinical manifestations of pathologically verified lacunar infarctions. *Stroke* 1989; **20**: 990-999

Wolf PA, D' Agostino RB, O'Neil MA, et al. Secular trends in stroke incidence and mortality: the Framingham study. *Stroke* 1992; **23**: 1551-1555

CHAPTER TWO

MEDICAL INTERVENTIONS IN
THE ACUTE PHASE OF STROKE

Prolonged focal brain ischaemia, as occurs in completed stroke, invariably leads to the development of an area of irreversible necrosis of brain tissue. Secondary brain injury may also ensue due to the effects of anoxia, cerebral oedema and diaschisis (see below). Although significant regeneration of nerve cells does not occur in the infarcted region, the human brain has an immense capacity to compensate for neuronal loss. Compensation for functional loss is achieved by a number of different mechanisms which may be enhanced by pharmacological and physical interventions, including behavioural training, in the acute and subacute phases of stroke. Understanding the processes that underlie neurological and functional recovery is an essential requisite for developing successful therapeutic strategies. This chapter summarises the current knowledge on how recovery occurs after stroke and describes the therapeutic interventions that may accelerate or retard this recovery.

THE MECHANISMS OF BIOLOGICAL RECOVERY FROM BRAIN INJURY
Following acute injury or disease of the central nervous system (CNS) predictable morphological, metabolic and biochemical processes occur mainly at the site and in the vicinity of the lesion. Favourable changes result in the partial or complete restoration of the anatomical and physiological integrity of the damaged neurones and their connections. Different mechanisms account for this recovery.

Biological recovery from stroke usually follows a stereotyped pattern and most of it occurs in the first 3-6 months. For example, the leg almost always recovers better than the upper limb following stroke in the territory of the middle cerebral artery and the improvement is first, as a rule, observed in the proximal part of the limb. Recovery is effected in the early stages by modulation of synaptic transmission and reversal of the consequences of secondary brain injury, i.e. restoration of perfusion in the ischaemic zone, resolution of ischaemia, anoxia, cerebral oedema and diaschisis. After the initial stages of stroke biological recovery is achieved by a process of tissue repair, i.e. regeneration. The final clinical outcome largely depends on the extent of recovery of the ischemic penumbra.

The ischaemic penumbra

Severe, prolonged cerebral ischaemia leads to the development of an area of cell necrosis. Between the boundaries of this area and the intact brain tissue lies a zone of reduced cerebral blood flow known as the ischaemic penumbra. The residual perfusion in the ischaemic penumbra is largely dependent on collateral circulation and is just enough to support the basic cellular metabolic function. The ischaemic penumbra can be visualised with positron emission tomographic (PET) scans. On the PET scan the penumbral zone corresponds to the brain region often described as the area of misery perfusion and is characterised by reduced regional cerebral blood flow with increased oxygen extraction fraction.

The initial stages of ischaemia are characterised by depletion of energy sources and severe impairment of the physiological function of neurones. The neurones become electrically silent and cease to exhibit spontaneous activity or generate evoked potentials. However, the membrane potential and the gross ionic homeostasis of these cells are still maintained. If the ischaemia is prolonged beyond a critical length of time, then the ionic homeostasis becomes disrupted. This causes the influx of sodium and calcium into the cell, the release of excitatory amino acids, cytotoxic oedema and irreversible damage of the structure and function of these neurones. However, recovery of the penumbral neurones is possible if perfusion is restored to an optimal level before cell necrosis occurs.

The metabolic state of the ischaemic penumbra is usually stable for a few hours and complete recovery of neurones in this area is often possible if the cerebral perfusion is restored (either spontaneously or with a therapeutic intervention) within a certain time window. In man the exact length of time during which the penumbral neurones can be salvaged is not known and appears to depend on the properties of the affected neurones. For example, hippocampal neurones appear to be more susceptible to ischaemic insult than cortical neurones. It is also possible that neuronal vulnerability to ischaemic damage varies from one person to another. In addition, a number of other factors may interfere with biological recovery and accelerate the neuronal death in the penumbral zone. These include pre-existing anaemia, profound systemic hypotension and anoxia. Pyrexia in the first 24 hours after stroke is also associated with poor functional recovery possibly because it accelerates the transformation of the ischaemic penumbra into an infarct. Clearly, the earlier the perfusion is restored, the better are the chances of recovery of the neurones in the ischaemic penumbra.

The ischaemic penumbra is potentially the most important substrate for early and late biological recovery following stroke and its rescue is one of the main objectives of the therapeutic interventions in the early phase of the cerebrovascular event. These interventions include thrombolysis, emergency carotid endarterctomy or angioplasty and neuroprotection. The aim is to restore the regional cerebral blood flow in the penumbral zone to an optimal level by medical or surgical means (revascularisation). Other therapeutic strategies include enhancing the collateral circulation by maintaining the systemic arterial blood pressure and by the use of drugs to increase the resistance of the penumbral neurones to the effects of ischaemia (neuroprotection).

The size of the ischaemic penumbra (which can be estimated in vivo with combined diffusion and perfusion MRI scans) correlates with the functional clinical outcomes after stroke, and as such may be useful in the prediction of the long-term prognosis in individual patients.

Cerebral oedema
Focal brain lesions, such as stroke, usually result in localised mild cerebral oedema that probably has no significant consequences for recovery. The effects of mild brain oedema are also transient, lasting on average about 3 weeks. However, rarely extensive and diffuse brain swelling may occur, usually following massive intracerebral haemorrhage or complete occlusion of the internal carotid or middle cerebral artery. Extensive oedema causes disturbances of cerebral function by two mechanisms. First, it can lead to displacement of brain structures, e.g. tonsilar herniation and brain stem compression. Secondly, it may cause generalised brain dysfunction such as epileptic seizures or reduced level of consciousness.

Diaschisis
Diaschisis (also known as functional deafferentation) is characterised by suppression of the neurophysiological and metabolic processes in regions adjacent to, or remote from the primary site of the infarcted area. These regions must be physiologically connected with the site of the lesion. In patients with hemiplegic stroke diaschisis has been demonstrated in the contralateral hemisphere and in the cerebellum. At least some of the early functional deficits after stroke can be explained by

diaschisis and its spontaneous reversal may account for some of the early biological recovery.

Reorganisation of cortical maps
More than a hundred years ago neurophysiological experiments have shown that each area of the cerebral cortex controls a specific neurological function. Although this concept of a rigid localisation of cerebral function subsequently proved to be an oversimplification, it generally holds true. For example, the comprehension of language resides in Wernicke area, whereas Broca's area is responsible for expressive language function. The early stimulation and ablation experiments have also demonstrated that the localisation of cerebral function is neither absolute, nor fixed. Fibre projections to one part of the cortex usually overlap with fibres from an adjacent region. These "somatotopic maps" are also capable of structural and functional re-organisation throughout life and this can occur at cortical and subcortical levels. Re-organisation of cortical maps is the primary mechanism that underlies spontaneous biological recovery. In the intact animal cortical maps are also altered by use and training that results in learning and acquisition of new motor and cognitive skills. In the early phase of recovery, two processes, namely unmasking and substitution, lead to changes in the cortical somatosensory maps.

Recent evidence suggests that reorganisation of cortical maps is mediated by two processes. One mechanism consists of changes in the dynamic balance between the excitatory and inhibitory neural circuits. It is thought that these changes lead to the unmasking and activation of latent neuronal pathways. The other process is the local modification of synaptic activity. Changes in the synaptic activity occur following lesions of the peripheral and central nervous system. The end result of these changes is that the responsiveness of partially denervated neurones is enhanced. This phenomenon is known as post-denervation supersensitivity and involves enhanced sensitivity of the receptors to the neurotransmitter. The number of the receptor also increases and, in addition, they may lose their specificity and become responsive to several neurotransmitters.

Unmasking - a given function is usually represented in the CNS in more than one brain area and can be executed by a group of neurones at different levels of the neuroaxis. These neurones are anatomically and functionally connected and higher centres normally inhibit those at lower levels. It has been suggested that in normal circumstances the lower centres act as a 'back up' system in a way similar to that of the pacemaker cells in the heart muscle. (Normally the sinus node is the cardiac pacemaker. However, failure of the sinus node to fire triggers the atrio-ventricular node to act as the primary cardiac impulse generator. With damage to the latter centre the idioventricular cells assume the role of the cardiac pacemaker). This hierarchical representation of neural function appears to be particularly important for recovery of motor function. Unmasking has been demonstrated with regional cerebral blood flow studies in patients with stroke.

Substitution - although each brain region, by and large, controls a specific functional activity, the cerebral localisation of neurological function is not absolute. Some brain structures have the capacity to mediate functions that are not normally attributed to them. This property is known as cerebral redundancy and has been mainly associated with recovery of language function. Neurones that mediate language function are in the dominant (usually the left) hemisphere. Transfer of language function to the non-dominant hemisphere following massive lesions of the classical language areas has been well documented. Biological recovery by substitution appears to be achieved by alternative latent neural pathways that have not been destroyed by the lesion.

Neural repair
Regeneration, i.e. restoration of the anatomical integrity of the injured axon, is the principal mechanism of repair in the peripheral nervous system. It is not an effective method of regeneration in the CNS. In the CNS anatomical and functional recovery is achieved by a process of pruning and collateral sprouting.

The process that results in repair of the damaged synaptic connections is called pruning if the new growth originates from the proximal part of the transected axon. On the other hand, when new synapses are formed by fibres from the intact neurones in the vicinity of the lesion, the process is referred to as collateral sprouting. Collateral sprouting is induced only in fibres that normally overlap the area destroyed by the lesion. Although the new fibres tend to retain the somatotopic organisation of those that they had replaced, projections to other sites may sometimes also occur. However, the significance of these aberrant connections is not fully understood. Pruning and collateral sprouting usually occur simultaneously and are seen within 6 weeks of the acute lesion.

FACTORS WHICH AFFECT BIOLOGICAL RECOVERY

The extent and tempo of biological recovery are influenced by many factors including the patient's age, site and size of the cerebral infarct, the subject's previous health and the presence or absence of other serious disease. Physical therapy (training) also plays an important role in recovery.

The patient's age appears to be important for recovery from stroke. Clinical observations suggest that the speed and pattern of clinical improvement in children is different from that of adults. In general stroke acquired early in childhood recovers faster and frequently with minimal residual focal neurological deficit. However, this is often associated with reduced overall cognitive development. In some cases recovery may be specific for only certain functions. For example, recovery from aphasia in children is usually better and faster than recovery from hemiplegia. The reverse is usually true for adults. Children also appear to tolerate cerebellar stroke better than adults. On the other hand, recovery from ischaemic lesions in the basal ganglia is often poorer in children than in adults.

The extent of damage to the anatomical structures caused by the stroke is also an important factor that influences recovery. Although there is no consistent linear relationship between the size of the lesion and the degree of biological recovery, extensive brain damage is often associated with poor functional outcomes. Poor health before the stroke has a similar effect. The standard of care in the acute phase of the cerebrovascular event has a significant influence on the extent of recovery from stroke. High quality and timely general supportive medical and nursing care is an essential requisite for promoting neuroplasticity and for creating the optimal conditions for functional recovery from stroke.

THE THERAPEUTIC INTERVENTIONS IN ACUTE STROKE

Medical care in the acute phase of stroke should aim to reduce mortality, to prevent or promptly reverse the early complications of stroke, and to create the optimal conditions for spontaneous and therapy-induced functional recovery.

GENERAL SUPPORTIVE CARE

The clinical outcomes of stroke are improved when general supportive medical care is started promptly and the patient's condition is meticulously monitored. Table 2.1 summarises the main interventions in the acute phase of stroke. Steps should be taken to maintain nutrition and hydration, prevent hypoxia, control the arterial blood pressure, and to ensure the adequate treatment of hyperglycaemia and hyperpyrexia without delay. Prevention of thromboembolic complications and skin pressure sores is also an important aspect of acute stroke care.

Hydration and nutrition

Dysphagia occurs in half the patients in the acute phase of stroke. However, most patients are able to swallow safely with the appropriate dietary modifications, the use of head posture and other manoeuvres to facilitate swallow, and with close monitoring during eating and drinking. In some cases, e.g. when a reduced level of consciousness or fatigue prevent adequate nutrition and hydration, the administration of intravenous fluids or feeding through a naso-gastric tube may be necessary for a few days. Insertion of a gastrostomy feeding tube should be considered if severe dysphagia to all food consistencies persists for more than 7-10 days (see chapter 3).

Normalisation of sleep

Sleep disorders are common after stroke. Poor sleep often reduces the patients' performance in physical and cognitive tasks by affecting memory, concentration and attention. Although spontaneous improvement of sleep may occur in a few weeks, many patients continue to be symptomatic in the long term and require treatment.

The management of insomnia should initially address the precipitating environmental factors, including ward noise, bright lights and low or high ambient temperatures. Emotional factors, such as anxiety, may also cause insomnia and may require specific interventions. If drug treatment is required, a non-benzodiazepine hypnotic, e.g. 3.75-7.5mg of zopiclone or 5mg of zolpidem, may be used for a short period. Overnight ventilation is indicated for sleep apnoea. Delivery of oxygen with a facial mask using a nasal continuous positive airway pressure (CPAP) machine is effective in most cases, but occasionally a tracheostomy may be required.

Correction of hypoxia

Hypoxia is common in acute stroke and can result from a number of complications. These include an abnormal central regulation of respiration, respiratory muscle weakness and reflex bronchospasm due to aspiration of food or fluid into the airways. Sleep-disordered breathing and sleep apnoea occur in more than half the patients with normal oxygen saturation while awake. These symptoms may persist for several weeks. Old age, lacunar strokes and pre-existing cerebrovascular disease are the main factors that predispose to sleep related disorders of breathing and nocturnal hypoxia.

Hypoxia in the acute phase of stroke can lead to neurological deterioration by accelerating neuronal death in the ischaemic penumbra. Arterial blood oxygen saturation should, therefore, be monitored with pulse oximetry in all patients on admission to hospital. Measurements of blood gases are indicated if the oxygen saturation on pulse oximetry is <95%. Patients with impaired level of consciousness and those with brain stem stroke are particularly vulnerable to hypoxia. These patients often require supplemental oxygen and, in some cases, intubation and artificial ventilation. Ventilatory support should also be considered in patients with cerebral oedema and raised intracranial pressure.

Early management of hypertension
Many patients are found to have a high blood pressure (BP) in the acute phase of stroke, but some present with profound hypotension. A high BP may be due to pre-existing hypertension or may occur de novo as a result of the cerebrovascular event itself. The stress associated with having a stroke or, less often, cerebral oedema can lead to a rise in BP. Acute urinary retention, faecal impaction or severe pain also have a similar effect. Hypertension due to these causes is usually transient and resolves when the underlying condition is adequately managed. Although the critical BP threshold that necessitates the use of antihypertensive medication is not known, it is generally accepted that a systolic BP ≤ 220 mm Hg or a diastolic BP ≤ 120 should not be treated in the first one or two weeks of acute stroke. There are, however, two exceptions. If the patient is due to undergo thrombolysis with tissue plasminogen activator (see below) or when there is evidence of hypertension-induced end organ damage, such as acute pulmonary oedema, hypertensive retinopathy or impairment of renal function, then rapid BP control is mandatory. In these circumstances intravenous labetalol is the treatment of first choice. The management of hypertension in the post-acute phase of stroke is discussed in chapter 6.

Correction of hypotension
In acute stroke hypotension may be due to cardiac arrhythmias or a coincidental acute myocardial infarction. These conditions can be either the cause of the stroke or, rarely, a complication

of it. Aggressive treatment of hypotension with blood volume expansion and the administration of vasopressors, e.g. dopamine or dobutamine, should not be delayed as prolonged hypotension has a deleterious effect on the ischaemic penumbra. The aim of treatment is to restore and maintain the BP at the upper limit of normal.

Treatment of hyperglycaemia
Hyperglycaemia is associated with a poor prognosis for recovery from stroke. Nonetheless, no intervention to correct the hyperglycaemia is usually required in the immediate aftermath of stroke in patients with a mild increase in their blood glucose. It is recommended that hyperglycaemia is treated if the blood glucose exceeds 16 mmol/l (300 mg/dl).

Treatment of hyperpyrexia
Fever in the first 24 hours of a cerebrovascular event usually occurs with large cerebral infarcts (or haemorrhages) and is associated with an increased morbidity and mortality rate in the early days after stroke. Frequently hyperpyrexia is due to a respiratory or urinary tract infection. However, in some patients it is due to the stroke itself. The control of hyperpyrexia with antipyretics or cooling has been shown in animal experiments to reduce the transformation of the ischaemic penumbra into an infarct.

Prevention of deep vein thrombosis and pressure sores
Immobility, dehydration and a flaccid muscle tone in the paralytic leg predispose to the development of deep vein thrombosis and pulmonary thromboembolism. However, although drug prophylaxis of DVT, e.g. with subcutaneous heparin injections, is usually effective, this strategy is associated with a high risk of intracerebral haemorrhage and bleeding in other organs. The routine use of pressure stockings is a safer alternative. Although full length and knee length thrombo-embolism deterrent (TED) stockings are widely used in clinical practice, it is not clear which of the two affords better protection against DVT.

Most stroke patients have a severely reduced mobility in the acute stage of their illness. This increases their risk of developing skin pressure sores. Other factors that predispose to this complication are a reduced level of consciousness, severe sensory impairment, urinary or faecal incontinence, cognitive impairment and a previous history of pressure sores. The skin of these patients should be examined at least daily and special attention should be given to the inspection of the skin over bony prominences and skin areas that are normally vulnerable to pressure damage. These are the heels, sacrum, ischeal tuberosity, femoral trochantors and elbows.

Regular skin inspection and risk assessment are important in the prevention and treatment of skin pressure sores. Although pressure sore risk assessment scales, such as the Waterlow scale, are widely used, these are not a substitute for the clinical examination. Persistent skin redness that does not blanch on pressure, blisters, localised swelling or heat or skin discolouration are vital signs of impending pressure sores.

The skin of patients with a high risk for pressure sore should be kept clean and dry at all times. The insertion of a urinary catheter may be necessary in some cases of urinary incontinence. Pressure on vulnerable skin areas should be minimised by correct positioning and periodic turning of the patient in bed and by the use of pressure-relieving devices, such as mattresses and cushions. Skin friction and shear damage should be avoided during turning the patient in bed or during transfers from chair to bed etc.

Table 2.1
Summary of the main therapeutic interventions in acute stroke

Symptom	What to do
Dysphagia	Dietary modification $\pm$ i.v. fluid supplements if dysphagia is mild. In severe dysphagia start nasogastric tube feeding. If severe dysphagia persists >7-10 days, consider insertion of a gastrostomy tube
Hypoxia	Oxygen saturation <95% - give oxygen by mask or nasal canula. Consider assisted ventilation in cases of respiratory failure or severe cerebral oedema
Hypertension systolic BP $\geq$ 220 or diastolic BP $\geq$ 120	Empty bladder, treat constipation & pain, then observe. Treat hypertension if: a) patient is a candidate for thrombolysis, or b) there is evidence of hypertensive end organ damage
Hypotension	Treat cause, e.g. volume depletion, arrhythmia etc. Raise BP to upper limit of normal with volume expanders $\pm$ dobutamine
Fever	Lower body temperature to normal.
Hyperglycaemia	Treat with insulin if blood glucose >16 mmol/l

In addition to the basic supportive care described above, direct measures to prevent the death of neurones in the ishaemic penumbra should be attempted, whenever possible. Salvage of the ischaemic penumbra may be achieved by restoring the penumbral blood flow and by increasing the resistance of the penumbral neurones to the effects of ischaemia, i.e. neuroprotection.

RESCUE OF THE ISCHAEMIC PENUMBRA
Spontaneous, usually partial, revascularisation of the occluded artery often occurs within hours or days after stroke and, together with the perfusion from the collateral circulation, helps to reverse the effects of ischaemia in the penumbral zone. This accounts for the spontaneous neurological improvement in the early phase of stroke. The effectiveness of the collateral circulation depends on the regional perfusion pressure which is normally proportional to the systemic arterial blood pressure. Therefore, systemic hypotension should be avoided and, as mentioned earlier, it is safer to withhold antihypertensive treatment in the early period after stroke in patients with a mild or moderate increase in blood pressure, especially if there is no evidence of previous hypertension (see chapter 6). In recent years it has become possible, in some cases, to reverse the effects of the reduced focal cerebral blood flow due to ischaemic stroke with intravenous or intra arterial thrombolysis. Improved perfusion of the ischaemic zone may also be possible with emergency carotid endarterectomy in those with critical stenosis of the cervical portion of the internal carotid artery.

Thrombolysis
The only thrombolytic agent that is approved for clinical use in stroke at present is alteplase or tissue plasminogen activator (tPA). Treatment with tPA (0.9 mg/kg body weight) is effective if the drug is given intravenously within 3 hours of the stroke onset and it is most beneficial in patients with a mild or moderate neurological deficit. The ischaemic aetiology of stroke must be confirmed with brain imaging and, in hypertensive patients, it is also essential to lower the systolic BP to <185 and the diastolic to <110 mm Hg before the administration of tPA. The main complication of thrombolysis with tPA is bleeding and the risk is highest in older patients and in those with severe neurological deficits on presentation. Neurological deterioration due to the development of vasogenic oedema or from the haemorrhagic transformation of the infarct may also occur. The contra indications to thrombolysis include a previous intracranial haemorrhage, myocardial infarction or severe traumatic brain injury in the 3 months preceding the stroke, major bleeding or surgery 3 weeks or less before the stroke or early post-stroke epileptic seizures.

Emergency carotid endarterectomy

Carotid endareterectomy (CE) may be considered in patients who present with a fluctuating or progressive neurological deficit in the first few hours of an ischaemic anterior circulation stroke, if they have 70% or more stenosis of the extracranial portion of the internal carotid artery ipsilateral to the cerebral infarct. Patients with acute occlusion of the internal carotid artery are also possible candidates for this procedure, irrespective of the course of the neurological deficit. Severely reduced level of consciousness, occlusion of the stem of the middle cerebral artery or an infarct size greater than 2.5cm in diameter are considered contra indications to emergency CE.

Neuroprotection

Cerebral ischaemia disrupts cellular homeostasis and, when prolonged, ultimately causes neuronal death. The events that lead to irreversible neuronal damage include the influx of calcium into the cell, the release of the excitatory amino acids aspartate, glutamate and glycine and the formation of oxygen free radicals. It is possible to block the different stages of this cascade of events. This intervention (which is known as neuroprotection) does not alter the cerebral perfusion in the penumbral zone but aims to improve the tissue tolerance to the effects of ischaemia. Hypothermia also appears to have a similar effect. However, hypothermia has no useful role in the management of acute stroke as the complications of this intervention usually outweigh its potential benefits. Cooling to achieve neuroprotection (i.e. core body temperature of $32\pm1°C$ for 48-72 hours) is frequently associated with fatal complications, including bronchopneumonia, cardiac arrhythmias and gastrointestinal haemorrhage.

Numerous neuroprotective agents have been developed. The list includes clomethiazole (gamma aminobutyric acid agonist), nimodipine (calcium antagonist) and selfotel (glutamate antagonist). These and other neuroprotective agents have been shown to prevent the deleterious effects of ischaemia on penumbral neurones in rats and other animal species. However, when used in the treatment of patients with acute stroke they were not found to be better than a placebo. At present neuroprtection has no place in the routine management of acute stroke

Stroke due to spontaneous arterial dissection

At present there is no agreement on the best method of treatment of dissection of the internal carotid and vertebral arteries and their intracranial branches. The current treatment options include the use of antithrombotic drugs, oral anticoagulation with warfarin, systemic or local intra-arterial thrombolysis with tissue plasminogen activator (t-PA), and stent angioplasty.

Most clinicians use antithrombotic drugs routinely in the treatment of spontaneous arterial dissection, as aspirin has been shown to be as effective as warfarin in these patients. The role of thrombolysis with t-PA is also limited because it may enlarge the arterial wall haematoma more than it dissolves the intra-arterial thrombus. The prognosis of carotid and vertebral artery dissection is usually good and it is probably sufficient to continue the antithrombotic treatment for 3-6 months only. However, rarely the symptoms of arterial dissection progress or recur after initial recovery. In these circumstances endovascular stent angioplasty may be considered.

MANAGEMENT OF STROKE COMPLICATIONS
IN THE ACUTE PHASE
Cardiac complications
Acute myocardial ischaemia and cardiac rhythm disturbances may occur as a result of stroke. Stroke in the region of the insula of the right cerebral hemisphere, in particular, is associated with cardiac arrhythmias and early sudden death. This is thought to be due to the importance of the insula in the regulation of the cardiac autonomic function. The cardiac function of patients with a large stroke, especially in the right middle cerebral artery territory, should be monitored carefully and any significant arrhythmia should be treated promptly.

Cerebral oedema
Massive cerebral oedema after stroke is usually seen in patients with complete occlusion of the internal carotid or middle cerebral artery. It tends to occur more often in young patients and is usually more severe than in older subjects, possibly because the brain atrophy associated with advanced age partially protects older patients from the effects of brain swelling. Typically, the patient presents with a dense hemiplegia and gaze palsy and is initially alert. However, within 24-48 hours the level of consciousness deteriorates and the patient develops signs of transtentorial herniation. (These are: third nerve palsy, Cheyne-Stokes respiration, bradycardia and coma). The extent of the brain swelling and the degree of shift of midline structures are readily demonstrable on brain imaging with a CT head scan. Extensive cerebral oedema is a life threatening condition that

requires prompt and aggressive management. Conservative management consists of the use of hyperosmolar solutions (e.g. i.v. mannitol 0.25-0.5 g/kg body weight over 20 minutes, 6-hourly), barbiturates and hyperventilation. The head of the bed should be elevated 20-30 degrees to facilitate venous drainage. The use of corticosteroids is of little or no value and appears to afford only a marginal improvement in the short-term survival and the functional outcome.

The benefits of the medical treatment of cerebral oedema are usually modest and transient. Unfortunately, even with early and aggressive intervention the mortality rate in patients with severe cerebral oedema is in the range of 80%. Emergency decompressive craniotomy may save life when the above-mentioned measures are unsuccessful or the patient's neurological status continues to deteriorate despite maximal conservative treatment. However, the decision to proceed with decompressive craniotomy should be made after careful consideration, as most patients who survive are left with severe long-term disability.

Post-stroke epilepsy
Epileptic seizures occur in approximately 3-4% of acute strokes either at the onset or within the first 24 hours. Their incidence is much higher in patients with lobar intracerebral haemorrhage than in those who have a basal ganglia haemorrhage or an ischaemic stroke. Simple or complex partial seizures with or without secondary generalisation account for the majority of post-stroke epilepsy and non-convulsive epilepsy may also occur. Generalised status epilepticus or epilepsia partialis continua may develop in about 15% of patients with early onset seizures. Early seizures are a strong predictor for subsequent seizures. Late onset epilepsy, i.e. seizures occurring after the first 4 weeks of stroke, is also common. About 10% of stroke patients develop epilepsy in the first year.

Anticonvulsant therapy with one drug is usually sufficient for the control of post-stroke seizures in the majority of patients. Sodium valproate is the drug of first choice for those with generalised seizures, whereas carbamazepine or oxcarbazine are the first-line treatment for those with simple or complex partial seizures with or without secondary generalisation. Treatment should be started with a small dose to reduce the possibility of drug adverse effects. The dose should then be titrated up slowly until optimal seizure control is achieved. Add-on therapy, e.g. with lamotrigine or gabapentin, may be required in a few patients with seizures resistant to maximum doses of the first line drugs. Phenytoin is no longer considered a first-line anticonvulsant and should be avoided, as some anecdotal evidence suggests that it may interfere with recovery from stroke.

Some stroke patients develop status epilepticus. The patient is said to be in status epilepticus if, for 30 minutes or more, the generalised or partial seizure activity continues or if the patient with recurrent (but not continuous) seizures does not recover consciousness between the fits. Status epilepticus is a major and life-threatening neurological emergency and requires prompt management. Hypoxia and hypoglycaemia, if present, should be corrected without delay. Intravenous lorazepam (4mg over 2 minutes) or diazepam (10mg over 2 minutes, then 5mg, if necessary to a maximum of 20mg). Resuscitation facilities should be available, as the benzodiazepines may cause respiratory arrest. If the seizures continue phenytoin infusion should be given in a dose of 15mg/kg at a rate of 50mg/minute. General anaesthesia may be needed to reverse the status epilepticus in some patients.

MANIPULATION OF BIOLOGICAL AND FUNCTIONAL RECOVERY WITH DRUGS

The majority of stroke patients take various medications for co-incidental medical disorders, such as hypertension, angina pectoris or mood disorders. The drugs that are used for these and other indications may have either a beneficial, neutral or deleterious effect on recovery from stroke. Most of the currently available data on the effects of drugs on neural plasticity are derived from animal experiments and their relevance to the recovery from stroke in humans is not fully understood. Nonetheless, it is imperative that drugs that are known or suspected of interfering with functional recovery are not prescribed to stroke patients whenever possible.

Experimental evidence suggests that central monoamine neurotransmission is important for recovery of neurological function after stroke. Drugs that enhance central alpha adrenoceptor or dopaminergic activity or inhibit the effects of gamma aminobutyric acid (GABA) have been shown to promote plasticity in the CNS and enhance motor recovery in animals. The opposite is also true. For example, it has been shown that infusion of noradrenaline into the cerebral ventricles of rats with experimentally-induced acute brain lesions results in faster and more complete recovery. On the other hand, depletion of noradrenaline (with a neurotoxin) impedes recovery.

It is not fully clear how drugs mediate their effect on neurological recovery. Possible mechanisms include the modulation of central neurotransmission, correction of the metabolic and functional consequences of diaschisis and effects on mental alertness and motivation.

Of the commonly used drugs clonidine, prazosin, the benzodiazepines, phenytoin, dopamine antagonists, neuroleptics and the antidepressant trazodone were shown to slow recovery in laboratory animals. Furthermore, these drugs caused new neurological deficits when given to animals that have recently recovered from experimentally-induced stroke. By contrast, bromocriptine, apomorphine, piracetam, lithium, desipramine and nimodipine accelerated recovery (see tables 2.2 and 2.3). Carbamazepine, fluoxetine and amitriptyline do not appear to have any significant effect on neurological recovery.

Table 2.2
Drugs that possibly promote neurological recovery

Mode of action	Examples
α1 adrenergic	amphetamine
Dopamine agonists	Bromocriptine, apomorphine
Unknown mechanism	Piracetam, lithium, nimodipine

Table 2.3
Drugs that possibly interfere with neurological recovery

Mode of action	Examples
α1 adrenergic blockers	Prazocin, doxazocin, terazocin
α2 adrenergic agonists	Clonidine
Dopamine antagonists	Haloperidol and neuroleptics
GABA agonists	Benzodiazepines
Unknown mechanism	Phenytoin, trazodone

Drugs may also be prescribed specifically to enhance neurological recovery. Preliminary evidence suggests that bromocriptine and piracetam may improve functional outcomes in dysphasic patients (see chapter 3). Amphetamines, when given in small doses and started early after the stroke, have also been reported to enhance motor recovery, especially when combined with task-specific training. However, the use of these drugs cannot be recommended for routine clinical use until further evidence for their effectiveness becomes available.

RECOMMENDED FURTHER READING

CNS plasticity
Cohen LG, Brasil-Neto JP, Pascual-Leone A, Hallett M. Plasticity of cortical motor output organisation following deafferentation, cerebral lesions, and skill acquisition. *Advances in Neurology* 1993; **63**: 187-200

Jacobs KM, Donoghue JP. Reshaping the cortical motor map by unmasking latent intracortical connections. *Science* 1991; **251**: 944-947

Karni A, Meyer G, Jezzard P, Adams MM, Turner R, Ungerleider LG. Functional MRI evidence for adult motor cortex plasticity during motor skill learning. *Nature* 1995; **377**: 155-158

Kozlowski DA, James DC, Schallert T. Use-dependent exaggeration of neuronal injury after unilateral sensorimotor cortex lesions. *Journal of Neuroscience* 1996; **16**: 4776-4786

Sanes JN, Donoghue JP, Thangaraj V, Edelman RR, Warach S. Shared neural substrates controlling hand movements in human motor cortex. *Science* 1995; **268**: 1775-1777

Weiller C, Chollet F, Friston KJ, Wise RJ, Frackowiak RS. Functional reorganisation of the brain in recovery from striatocapsular infarction in man. *Annals of Neurology* 1992; **31**: 463-472

Goldstein LB. Potential effects of common drugs on stroke recovery. *Archives of Neurology* 1998; **55**: 454-456

The ischaemic penumbra
Castillo J, Davalos A, Marrugat J, Noya M. Timing for fever-related brain damage in acute ischaemic stroke. *Stroke* 1998; **29**: 2455-2460

Karonen JO, Vanninen RL, Liu Y et al. Combined diffusion and perfusion MRI with correlation to single-photon emission CT in acute ischaemic stroke. Ischaemic penumbra predicts infarct growth. *Stroke* 1999; **30**: 1583-1590

Baird AE, Dambrosia J, Janket S-J et al. A three-item scale for the early prediction of stroke recovery. *Lancet* 2001; **357**: 2095-2099

Neuroprotection
Li Q, Stephenson D. Postischemic administration of basic fibroblast growth factor improves sensorimotor function and reduces infarct size following permanent focal cerebral ischemia in the rat. *Experimental Neurology* 2002; **177**: 531-537

Bogousslavsky J, Victor SJ, Salinas EO et al. Fiblast (trafermin) in acute stroke: results of the European-Australian phase II/III safety and efficacy trial. *Cerebrovascular Disease* 2002; **14**: 239-251

Dorman PJ, Counsell CE, Sandercock PAG. Recently developed neuroprotective therapies for acute stroke. *CNS Drugs* 1996; **6**: 457-474

Medical and surgical treatments

Adams Jr,HP, Adams RJ, Brott J et al. Guidelines for the early management of patients with ischaemic stroke. *Stroke* 2003; **34**: 1056-1083

The National Institute of Neurological Disorders, and Stroke rt-PA Stroke Study Group. Tissue plasminogen activator for acute ischaemic stroke. *New England Journal of Medicine* 1995; **333**: 1581-1587

Morley NCD, Berge E, Cruz-Flores S, Whittle IR. Surgical decompression for cerebral oedema in acute ischaemic stroke (Cochrane Review). The Cochrane Library 2003; issue 3. Oxford: Update Software; 2003

CHAPTER THREE

MANAGEMENT OF THE COMMON IMPAIRMENTS ASSOCIATED WITH STROKE

Stroke usually results in multiple impairments that develop simultaneously. These occur in various combinations depending on the site and size of the brain lesion. Dominant hemisphere strokes usually cause aphasia, apraxia, hemiplegia and hemianopia. Hemispatial neglect is more common and more severe in patients with non-dominant hemisphere stroke and severe hemisensory loss usually develops as a result of a thalamic haemorrhage or infarct. Diplopia, ataxia and dysarthria are characteristic features of brain stem or cerebellar stroke. All strokes, irrespective of their location, may result in dysphagia.

LANGUAGE AND SPEECH DISORDERS

DYSPHASIA

The terms dysphasia and aphasia are usually used interchangeably to mean impairment of language comprehension, expression or both. Dysphasia results from lesions in the specific areas of the dominant cerebral hemisphere that are described below. Thus, the definition of dysphasia excludes the language disorders that result from global intellectual impairment (severe learning disability or dementia), deafness or disorders of phonation. Language is the formulation and conveying of one's thoughts in words and sentences and should be distinguished from speech. The latter is the articulation of language. Dysphasia often co-exists with verbal (articulatory) dyspraxia – a disorder of the preparation and execution of speech.

Dysphasia (or aphasia) is one of the commonest neurological deficits following stroke. Approximately one-third of those who survive the initial vascular event have a significant impairment of their language function. The impact of dysphasia on these patients and their families is often considerable. About 30-40% of subjects with a dominant hemisphere stroke resulting in expressive dysphasia experience profound depressive symptoms. Although depression may be independent of the language disturbance in some patients, dysphasia remains one of the strongest predictors of depression in the stroke population as a whole. Dysphasia also increases the level of dependency of stroke patients on their carers and may even make admission to institutional care the only safe option for some patients even when the other symptoms and signs of stroke have completely resolved.

The successful management of dysphasic patients requires the accurate diagnosis of the type of the language disorder, the assessment of its severity, and the exclusion of other conditions that can mimic dysphasia. The assessment of the patient's cerebral dominance for language and his level of formal education may provide valuable prognostic information.

The anatomical organisation of language function

Both cerebral hemispheres are involved in language function. An oversimplified account of the lateralisation of language function is that instinctive language that conveys emotions and non-verbal communication, such as gestures and facial expression, is subserved by neurones in the hypothalamus and both cerebral hemispheres. By contrast, propositional language, i.e. the processes of inner thought and their external expression in spoken and written language, is associated with the left (dominant) hemisphere in right-handed people and in most ambidextrous and left-handed individuals.

The primary language areas are concentrated around the Sylvian fissure of the dominant hemisphere. Anteriorly, in the inferior frontal gyrus between the anterior and ascending rami of the Sylvian sulcus, is Broca's area. Broca's area is responsible for expressive language function. Wernicke area is found in the posterior part of the first (superior) temporal convolution. This is the receptive language area and is essential for language comprehension. The classical Broca's and Wernicke areas are not the only brain regions responsible for expressive and receptive language function. In fact, isolated lesions of these areas usually result in a relatively mild and transient dysphasia and involvement of the insula and the operculum adjacent to these structures is typically present in severe and moderately severe cases. The expressive and receptive language areas are joined together by two bundles of fibres: the arcuate fasciculus and the superior longitudinal fasciculus. Other perisylvian language areas are the supramarginal and angular gyri in the anterior and middle parts of the inferior parietal lobule, respectively.

The classical language areas receive their blood supply from the middle cerebral artery (MCA). As shown in the table below, the vascular territory affected by stroke in a given patient can be predicted from the type of dysphasia.

61

Table 3.1
The vascular territories involved in the different types of dysphasia

Type of dysphasia	Vascular territory
Broca'a	Left MCA, upper division
Wernicke's	Lower division of left MCA
Global	Internal carotid or stem of left MCA
Conduction	Ascending parietal or posterior temporal branch of left MCA
Transcortical (motor or sensory)	Watershed infarct

The clinical features of dysphasia

The language deficit in dysphasia may involve any component of the linguistic system, i.e. the phonological (sounds that form words), morphological-lexical (word form), syntactic (grammar) or semantic component (word meaning). In all, but mild cases, the rate and rhythm of the patient's verbal output are frequently disrupted and the speech may contain paraphasic errors. In addition, the construction of sentences may become grammatically incorrect (agrammatism). In very mild dysphasia the language impairment may consist only of word-finding difficulties (anomia).

Verbal fluency is decreased in expressive dysphasia. Speech is sparse and in severe cases it is completely or almost completely absent. Some dysphasic patients produce stereotyped utterances. These may be correct words or non-words that are repeated several times whenever the patient attempts to speak. Dysprosody is also common and is characterised by slow, monotonous speech. Verbal fluency may be increased in receptive dysphasia.

Paraphasia is an important feature of dysphasia and results from disruption at the phonological, lexical or semantic levels of language organisation. Letters in a word may be omitted, added or substituted (literal or phonemic paraphasia) or a word may be replaced by a conceptually similar one, e.g. chair – stool, pen - pencil. This is known as semantic paraphasia. Sometimes patients invent new words that did not exist in their language (neologism). These aberrations usually occur in different combinations. When paraphasia, agrammatism and neologism are present together the patient is said to have jargon aphasia.

Classification of dysphasia

Except in a few cases the type of dysphasia correlates closely with the site and the extent of the brain lesion. Consequently, the classification of dysphasia may be used in clinical practice to confirm the anatomical diagnosis and to predict the prognosis for recovery. It may also be useful to guide the choice of the therapy interventions. However, it should be recognised that the different syndromes of aphasia often overlap. Furthermore, there are often many variations in the patients' symptoms even within the same diagnostic category.

Dysphasia may be broadly classified into predominantly expressive or predominantly receptive type. The expressive (motor) dysphasias include classical Broca's, isolation, transcortical motor and global dysphasia and are characterised by severely reduced verbal fluency and dysprosody. (Dysprosody is a speech disorder characterised by monotony of pitch and loudness and reduced stress of syllables). Interestingly, well-learnt phrases such as prayers and emotional language, e.g. swearing, are often preserved. Comprehension in global and isolation dysphasia is severely impaired. Repetition is also poor in global dysphasia and this distinguishes it from isolation dysphasia. With the exception of cases of global dysphasia, patients with expressive language dysfunction usually have insight into their verbal communication disability and are often frustrated by it. Depression is common in these patients.

The receptive (sensory) dysphasias are Wernicke, transcortical sensory and conduction dysphasia. In these forms of dysphasia the language output is not altered or only slightly reduced. The deficit is primarily that of language comprehension. Language is fluent and contains numerous paraphasic and grammatical errors and jargon. Transcortical dysphasia (TCD) is characterised by poor auditory comprehension, severely reduced spontaneous propositional speech but excellent repetition (transcortical mixed dysphasia). When comprehension is relatively preserved the TCD is referred to as motor. The term sensory TCD implies the reverse. Patients with this disorder often demonstrate the "completion" phenomenon, i.e. the patient completes a sentence that is started by the examiner. The sentence would normally be a well-known phrase, a proverb or a song. The potential for verbal learning is usually preserved in all forms of this syndrome. In conduction dysphasia (or isolation of the speech area) the main symptom is poor repetition. In transcortical and conduction dysphasias the classical speech areas, i.e. Broca's and Wernicke areas and the arcuate fasciculus, are spared.

Verbal perseveration is usually associated with lesions of the head of the caudate nucleus and mutism with fronto-putamenal lesions. By contrast, disorders of naming and word-finding difficulties can result from damage to one or more of many cortical and subcortical structures and do not predict the site of the lesion. Extensive putamenal lesions are usually associated with hypophonia. The characteristic features of the main types of dysphasia and the site of the lesions responsible for each of them are summarised below (see table 3.2).

Table 3.2
The clinical classification of dysphasia

Aphasia	Site of lesion	Fluency	Comprehension	Repetition
Broca's	Left inferior frontal gyrus ± subcortical area, insula & operculum.	+++	0/ +	+++
Wernicke's	Left posterior temporal lobe, underlying white matter, ± insula.	0	+++	++
Global	As listed under Broca's & Wernicke dysphasia.	+++	+++	+++
Conduction	Left arcuate fasciculus & supramarginal gyrus.	0/+	0/+	+++
Transcortical motor	Frontal speech association areas.	+++	+++	0/+
Transcortical sensory	Deep temporo-parietal speech association areas.	0	+++	0/+
Transcortical mixed	Large lesions of speech association areas	+++	+++	0/ +

Key
+++ = severe impairment, ++ = moderate impairment, + = mild impairment, 0 = no impairment

Assessment of handedness and the level of formal education

The cerebral hemisphere where language function resides is known as the dominant hemisphere. In most people this is the left hemisphere. There is a strong correlation between lateralisation of language function to the left hemisphere and the person's preference to use his or her right hand in tasks that require the use of only one hand, such as writing or throwing a ball. Therefore, establishing the patient's hand preference (or handedness) may be used as a simple method for determining cerebral hemisphere dominance.

Knowledge of the cerebral hemisphere dominance for language in patients presenting with dysphasia provides useful prognostic information. The prognosis of aphasia appears to be better in patients with right hemisphere dominance. Left-handed subjects tend to become dysphasic regardless of which hemisphere is damaged and they often recover faster and more completely than dextral individuals.

Different methods have been devised to assess handedness. For routine clinical practice it is probably sufficient to determine handedness by recording the patient's responses to the following five questions: which hand they prefer to throw a ball with, to hold a toothbrush with, to cut bread with, to hold a spoon with and to strike a match with. Hand preference for writing and drawing should not be used as it is often influenced by cultural norms. A family history of sinistrality is also important. Those with a left-handed parent or sibling are also likely to be left-handed.

The patient's level of formal education also has a prognostic significance and seems to influence recovery from dysphasia. However, it is more relevant to propositional language than to instinctive language. Good performance in reading and writing tasks after dysphasia also correlates with high pre-morbid educational attainments.

Differential diagnosis

Parkinson's disease, depressive illness and dementia usually result in reduced verbal fluency and may be confused with expressive dysphasia. On the other hand, patients with receptive dysphasia may be misdiagnosed as having an acute mental confusional state, especially if there is no obvious hemiparesis. Neglect dyslexia and neglect dysgraphia (see the section on unilateral hemispatial neglect) and the disintegration of language function that occurs in dementia are sometimes mistaken for dysphasia. In all of these condition a detailed medical history and clinical examination are usually sufficient to confirm the diagnosis. Analysis of the language disorder is also helpful in the differential diagnosis, especially in cases of dementia and acute confusional states.

In dementia all aspects of language are impaired, but to a different degree. Demented patients do particularly badly in language tasks that demand sustained attention, abstract thinking or generalisation. In addition, the patients' vocabulary shrinks, their speech becomes stereotyped, simple and repetitious. On the other hand, the language dysfunction seen in those with acute toxic confusional states is characterised by poor and irrelevant information content and, in addition, there is always some evidence of disorientation and lack of clarity of thinking. Typically, the syntax and semantic aspects of language are not affected in these patients.

Language disorders associated with thalamic lesions
Discrete lesions of the dominant thalamus (usually the result of thalamic haemorrhage) may also cause language dysfunction. The dysphasia of thalamic origin is characterised by frequent semantic paraphasic errors, relatively preserved comprehension and repetition.

Language disorders associated with non-dominant hemisphere lesions
Subtle language deficits are often seen in patients with non-dominant hemisphere stroke. These include perseveration and spelling errors when reading and writing and are usually due to impaired scanning of the text or poor attention to the task. Dysporosody is frequently present and, in severe cases, the patient's ability to communicate efficiently may be affected. Inefficient communication in these subjects is characterised by a verbal output that contains redundant and irrelevant information and by failure to respond to contextual cues.

Bedside assessment of dysphasia
In addition to the dysphasia, other neurological deficits may be elicited on the standard physical examination. In particular, it is important to look for the presence of oro-buccal (facial) apraxia. Oro-buccal apraxia is very common in patients with left hemisphere lesions (see the section on limb apraxia) and has an important effect on the patient's language function. Once the

diagnosis of dysphasia is confirmed the next step in the patient's assessment is to determine the type, the severity of the language deficit and its impact on the patient's ability to communicate with others.

As stated above, the assessment of only three language characteristics is usually sufficient for the classification of the type of dysphasia. These are speech fluency, auditory comprehension and repetition. Fluency is tested by asking conversational questions and by requesting the patient to describe a simple picture. The evaluation should also include assessment of the information content of speech and its prosody. To test comprehension the patient is asked questions of increasing complexity. Repetition is tested by asking the subject to repeat numbers, words and sentences. The test should include words that are frequently used in everyday conversation as well as words that are rarely used. Prosody and speech volume are judged subjectively by the clinician. Disorders of reading and writing usually mirror the oral language deficits and are elicited by asking the patient to read a text, copy written material and to write to dictation.

Standardised assessment scales may be used when a formal evaluation of dysphasia is needed. There are several assessment scales, e.g. the Western Aphasia Battery and the Boston Diagnostic Aphasia Examination, that measure language function at the level of impairment. Some tests, such as the Communicative Effectiveness Index, measure the impact of dysphasia on the patient's every day function. A third group of standardised tests that are based on psycholinguistic models of dysphasia are also frequently used in clinical practice. These include PALPA (the Psycholinguistic Assessment of Language Processing in Aphasia) and CAT (the Comprehensive Aphasia Test).

Rehabilitation of dysphasic patients
Language is necessary for processing thoughts (i.e. we think through language) and also to enable communication between individuals for social interaction. The primary objective of treatment of dysphasia is to restore language function. However, complete functional recovery usually occurs in a relatively small number of patients. When recovery is limited the therapeutic interventions should aim to maximise the patient's residual language abilities and to facilitate non-verbal communication. This can be achieved by encouraging the patient to use gesture and other means including the use of various communication aids that range in sophistication from simple picture or letter

charts to electronic devices. Frequently, treatment strategies to improve verbal and non-verbal communication are used together. An important aspect of the care for aphasic patients is to educate their family members and carers on the nature of the patient's linguistic disability and to advise them on how best to communicate with the patient, both verbally and non-verbally.

Speech and language therapy
Training appears to have a specific positive effect on recovery of language function. Anecdotal observations suggest that spontaneous recovery of post stroke dysphasia occurs in the absence of specific speech and language therapy but there is also evidence that treatment may enhance recovery. Treatment seems to be most effective when therapy is started early and is given over at least the first 3 months after the stroke onset. Young patients with good insight into their verbal communication disability and those who attempt to correct their language errors without prompting tend to respond better to therapy.

A speech and language therapy session usually consists of practice on picture matching, naming objects, sentence completion, instructions to carry out tasks, conversations and the use of gesture and other means of non-verbal communications. As a rule, initially therapy is delivered on a one-to-one basis. As the patient's linguistic abilities improve he may be enrolled into a group therapy programme. Typically, the group consists of 6-8 patients and their carers with the therapist acting as a facilitator during the treatment session. The aim of group therapy is to improve the patient's functional communication, confidence and self-esteem and to promote the carer's understanding of the patient's linguistic disability. In recent years, computer-based speech and language therapy has become popular.

A common clinical observation is that some patients with expressive dysphasia are often reluctant to engage in conversation, possibly because of embarrassment or fear of failure. This may lead to learned non-use of language. In recent years a new treatment method of dysphasia known as constraint-induced therapy (CIT) has been suggested as a means to overcome learned non-use of language. CIT is based on games that force the patient to use speech and prohibit the use of non-verbal communication. The therapy programme, which typically consists of 30-35 hours of treatment over two weeks, is individualised to suite the patient's needs. It is introduced gradually and the complexity of the intervention is increased incrementally in accordance with the rules of the game. Preliminary reports suggest that CIT may improve verbal communication more than conventional therapy in patients with chronic dysphasia. However, this form of treatment has not yet been fully evaluated.

Augmentative and alternative communication (AAC)
Patients with expressive dysphasia (and good auditory comprehension) and those with severe dysarthria or dysphonia may benefit from systems that enhance or substitute verbal communication. A wide range of AAC aids exists and they are usually effective if chosen carefully. AAC systems have been shown to increase the interaction of dysphasic patients with their carers, improve their language skills and learning. Frequently, the sustainability of use of AAC devices, i.e. the continuation of their use after professional involvement stops, is determined by the patient's perception of the need for them and of their usefulness in different social contexts.

Drug treatment of dysphasia
Some case reports and the findings of a few open-label studies and small randomised, controlled trials suggest that the pharmacological treatment of dysphasia may enhance language recovery when combined with speech and language therapy. The drugs that have been reported to be effective include d-amphetamine, piracetam and bromocriptine. However, to date these reports have not been confirmed by large, well-designed, randomised, placebo-controlled studies.

Prognosis of dysphasia
The prognosis for recovery from severe dysphasia is generally poor. With the current methods of treatment only about 30% of patients with an infarct in the left middle cerebral or internal carotid artery territory show significant functional improvement or complete recovery at 3-6 months. The chances of recovery are much improved if the dysphasia is due to a thalamic lesion. Global dysphasia has the worst prognosis, whereas Broca's and Wernicke aphasia usually have an intermediate prognosis. Recovery from anomic, conduction, transcortical and subcortical dysphasias is usually excellent and, as a rule, is complete in a few weeks. Anomic dysphasia is a common end point in the evolution of most types of language disorders.

DYSARTHRIA
Dysarthria is a disorder of articulation of speech. Dysarthric speech is slurred, slow and imprecise. It is often monotonous and

dysprosodic. However, the speech is usually intelligible except in severe cases. In addition to the severity of stroke, intelligibility of dysarthric speech is often affected by other factors, such as fatigue and drowsiness.

Dysarthria is common after stroke and affects up to 30% of patients. The incidence is higher following posterior circulation stroke and brain stem and lacunar infarcts. It results from interruption of the motor cortico-bulbar pathways to the tongue and other oro-facial muscles, and from lesions of the brain stem (usually infarcts of the base of the pons or cerebral peduncle) or the cerebellum. Dysarthria in stroke patients may also result from causes other than the neurological lesion. These causes, which include ill-fitting dentures, mouth ulcers and oral thrush, should be recognised and managed as appropriate.

In routine clinical practice the presence of dysarthria and its severity are confirmed by listening to the patient during spontaneous speech or whilst reading a short text or repeating words or sentences on command. Slurring and dysprosody can usually be easily identified. The assessment should also include evaluation of the voice quality, pitch and intensity and the overall intelligibility of speech.

Different therapeutic strategies are used to improve intelligibility of speech in severely dysarthric patients. These include voice and prosody training and exercises to strengthen and improve the coordination of the oro-facial musculature. In some cases the use of protheses, e.g. palatal lift to compensate for hypernasal speech, may improve speech clarity. Various communication aids are also used.

LIMB APRAXIA
Ideomotor and ideational apraxia
Ideomotor apraxia is a cognitive deficit characterised by the inability to carry out a learned, purposeful motor activity in the absence of a significant muscle weakness, impairment of sensory function or poor comprehension of the required task. When the disability is partial the condition is referred to as dyspraxia. However, the terms apraxia and dyspraxia are often used interchangeably. Ideomotor apraxia is broadly classified into limb apraxia and oro-buccal (facial) apraxia. Sometimes the apraxic errors result from failure to follow the correct sequence of the different steps that are required to complete the motor task successfully. In these situations planning, rather than the

actual execution of the motor act, is primarily affected and the patient is said to have ideational apraxia. It is not clear whether ideational apraxia is a distinct clinical entity or whether it is a severe form of ideomotor apraxia.

Constructional and dressing apraxia

Constructional and dressing apraxia should not to be confused with limb apraxia. These disorders result from impairment of visual-spatial perception and are primarily associated with non-dominant parietal lobe lesions. Constructional apraxia is defined as the inability to assemble an object from its constituent parts. By contrast, dressing apraxia is characterized by difficulties with aligning the items of clothing to the appropriate part of the body. For example, a patient with dressing apraxia may insert his leg through a shirt sleeve while attempting to dress his upper body or put on a garment back-to-front.

Apraxic agraphia

Writing is a learned motor skill and is often disrupted in patients with limb apraxia. The disruption of writing that is not due to dysphasia, or motor or sensory impairment is known as apraxic agraphia. Apraxic agraphia is characterised by poor formation of letters which, in severe cases, results in an illegible scribble. Typically, letter imagery and oral spelling are intact. The patient is also able to write correctly using a keyboard of a typewriter or word processor.

There are no accurate data on the incidence and prevalence of apraxia in the stroke population. This is partly because the frequent co-existence of aphasia hampers the detailed assessment of these patients. Nonetheless, most studies estimate that one in three patients with a first-ever stroke develop apraxia. Limb apraxia is seen predominantly after left hemisphere lesions and its occurrence does not seem to correlate with the type of stroke (i.e. ischaemic or haemorrhagic) or with the patient's age or gender. Limb apraxia due to right hemisphere stroke is relatively rare and has an estimated incidence of less than 10%.

The pathogenesis of limb and oro-buccal apraxia

Apraxia has been explained on the basis of disconnection of the upper posterior part of the temporal lobe of the dominant hemisphere (Wernicke area) from the pre-frontal cortex. This hypothesis is based on the assumptions that there is a link between language and motor function and that the dominant (left) hemisphere is essential for the acquisition of motor skills and the execution of learned motor acts. Consequently, in order to execute a learned movement on command with the right hand the subject must first understand the command. Comprehension of language takes place in Wernicke's area. Information must pass from this area to the left premotor region and then to the origin of the pyramidal tract in the left precentral gyrus. Commands to carry out a motor task with the left hand are processed through the same pathway and are then relayed to the right precentral gyrus via the corpus callosum. Therefore, limb apraxia usually results from a lesion in the left hemisphere. The lesion must destroy the lower parietal lobe (thus isolating Wernicke area from the motor cortex) or damage the premotor area. A lesion in the anterior part of the corpus callosum (at its origin in the left premotor area or in the midline) may also cause apraxia.

Although facial movements have bilateral cortical representation, facial (orobuccal) apraxia is very common. It results from lesions of the left premotor region because these lesions destroy the precentral face area and also the callosal fibres at their origin. These lesions do not affect axial movements (movements of the eyes, neck or trunk) which are thought to be subserved by non-pyramidal pathways and are under bilateral cortical control. Apraxia after stroke seldom occurs as an isolated phenomenon. Table 3.3 summarises the relationship between the site of the lesion and the apraxic syndromes.

Table 3.3
The effects of the site of the lesion on the clinical presentation in apraxia

Site of lesion/ vascular territory	Apraxic syndrome
Left parietal lobe – middle cerebral artery	Apraxia of both limbs & face, conduction aphasia, no hemiplegia.
Left premotor area – middle cerebral artery	Apraxia of both limbs & face, Broca's aphasia, right hemiplegia.
Corpus callosum – anterior cerebral, peri-callosal artery	Unilateral left apraxia with or without agraphia & tactile anomia of left hand.

The clinical aspects of limb apraxia

The hallmark of limb apraxia is the patient's inability to complete a learned motor task successfully. This may be due to difficulties with planning of the functional activity, or with the initiation or the execution of the components of the task in the correct sequence. Any or all of these stages can be affected in an apraxic patient. In addition, apraxic patients also often have difficulties with the manipulation of objects. The patient may make errors with the selection of the tools and objects that are required to carry out the task. Alternatively, he may choose the appropriate object but fails to use it correctly or applies it to the wrong part of the body.

Normally, patients with limb apraxia do not report their difficulties with the execution of learned motor skills. This could be explained, at least in part, by the frequent co-occurrence of dysphasia in these patients. Traditionally, screening for apraxia is made by asking the patient to carry out a learned motor act on command, to imitate gestures and to demonstrate the use of common tools and objects. However, there is often a poor correlation between the patients' performance on the pantomimed use of tools and objects and their actual ability to use the same tools and objects in real life situations. The diagnosis of apraxia and the assessment of its severity are, therefore, best evaluated by observing the patient's performance when carrying out activities of daily living (ADL).

Diagnosis

Observation by an experienced clinician of the patient's performance of ADL is probably the most reliable method of diagnosis of apraxia. The diagnosis may be supported by bedside tests as described below.

Ideational apraxia is tested by asking the patient to demonstrate the use of objects to carry out a given task, for example to clean his teeth with a toothbrush. The subject's performance of the different constituent parts of the task and the order in which they are performed are assessed. The objective is to test the patient's ability to plan the motor act. To test for ideomotor apraxia (i.e. difficulties with implementation of motor plans) the patient is asked to imitate gestures, for instance to mime the act of cleaning his teeth with a toothbrush. Meaningful and meaningless gestures may be used and tests that combine the use of gesture and movement copying appear to be the most useful. Patients may fail in these tests because they are not able to recognise objects. Screening for agnosia (e.g. with a test to pick the 'odd one out') should therefore precede the assessment for apraxia. Similarly, the patient's ability to understand the clinician's instructions should be confirmed by excluding the presence of clinically significant receptive dysphasia.

In an attempt to standardise the bedside assessment scales of apraxia, van Heugten et al (see the list of recommended further reading) have recently proposed a new scale. This scale is made of two subsets - the demonstration of the use of objects and imitation of gesture.

In the first part of the test the subject is asked to demonstrate the use of nine objects under three different test conditions (see table 3.4 below). The responses are scored as follows: for the correct selection and appropriate use of the object the patient scores 3 points. Two points are awarded if the performance on the task resembles the correct one, but is imprecise. The patient scores 1 point if only part of the task is completed successfully. Total failure to accomplish the task is scored as zero.

Table 3.4
Diagnosis of apraxia - use of objects

Object	Test condition
Key, hammer, toothbrush	Verbal command only. Object not shown
Spoon, hammer, scissors	Object shown, but subject may not touch it
Eraser, comb, screwdriver	The actual use of object is tested

In addition to the use of objects, the patient is instructed to imitate the following gestures: sticking his tongue out, blowing out a candle, closing his eyes, waving goodbye, saluting, and making a fist. The maximum score for each item of the subsets is 6 points (54 points for use of objects and 36 for imitation of gesture, total score = 90). A score of 83 or less suggests the diagnosis of apraxia.

Treatment

The impact of limb apraxia on the patient's functional abilities is often considerable. The presence of severe limb apraxia correlates with high levels of dependency in activities of daily living. In addition, it may limit the ability of the individual to use alternative strategies to compensate for motor impairments. It also often interferes with the successful acquisition of new motor skills during rehabilitation.

Rehabilitation of apraxia has not received much attention in the past and to date there are no universally accepted and successful treatment methods of this disorder. The traditional approach to the treatment of limb apraxia is a reiterative, problem-solving educational process that is underpinned by repeated practice of the deficient motor skill. Relearning to perform motor tasks has been shown to occur with this therapeutic strategy. However, treatment of one error type usually does not generalise to improvement for other types of apraxic errors. To overcome this problem it is important that the therapeutic intervention is directed to remediate specific error items that have functional relevance to patients and their carers.

More recently, preliminary evidence suggests that a method known as 'strategy training' may be effective. This treatment approach is based on the selection of specific functional goals for the individual patient. The interventions are then tailored to address these goals while taking account of the patient's level of functional disability. A hierarchical method of instructions, assistance and feedback are used. Initially, the patient may be asked verbally to carry out the task. If he is unsuccessful, then the therapist gives verbal and non-verbal cues. When the patient fails again to accomplish the task, the therapist proceeds, in this order, to assist through gestures, then by demonstrating the task, and, finally, by giving 'hands on' assistance. Assistance is gradually withdrawn as the patient's functional abilities increase. (For more details on 'strategy training' see van Heugen et. al. 1998 quoted in the list of further reading).

UNILATERAL HEMISPATIAL NEGLECT

A significant number of patients develop cognitive deficits as a result of their stroke. Unilateral hemispatial sensory neglect is probably the commonest and clinically one of the most important cognitive impairments in these patients.

Unilateral hemispatial sensory neglect (also called hemineglect, visual neglect, visual inattention) is a complex and multi-faceted phenomenon that is characterised by loss of spatial awareness. It appears to be primarily due to impairment of selective attention, although other cognitive processes may be involved. Unilateral hemispatial neglect (UHN) is defined as the total or partial failure of spontaneous selective orientation to objects or attention to novel, meaningful stimuli arising in the space contralateral to the side of the brain lesion despite intact peripheral sensation. Consequently, the patient does not direct his attention to these stimuli or responds to them. The stimuli may be visual, auditory or tactile. Sometimes a patient with mild hemiparesis and relatively good motor function exhibits difficulties with the execution of goal-directed movements or does not use the affected limb spontaneously for tasks in the neglected hemispace. This is known as motor neglect. Unilateral hemispatial neglect may be associated with impairments of non-lateralised attention, i.e. deficits in sustained attention and reduced general alertness. Similarly, a primary sensory deficit, e.g. hemianopia, may co-exist. Hemiplegia or hemiparesis are also frequently present.

Patients with UHN ignore stimuli arising in the horizontal (left-to-right) plane. UHN may occur in relation to the patient's body (body-centered neglect) or in relation to the objects in the neglected hemispace (object-centered neglect). Body-centered neglect is classified into:
a) Neglect of personal body space, i.e. neglect of the affected half of the body
b) Neglect of peripersonal space. (The peripersonal space is defined here as the space within the patient's arm reach).
c) Neglect of far space.
Any one, or any combination of these types of neglect may be present in the same patient. Object-centered neglect occurs less frequently. Whereas body-centered neglect is strongly lateralised, the patient with object-centered neglect ignores the left (or right) half of objects irrespective of where they are in space.

The phenomena associated with unilateral hemispatial neglect

Patients with UHN often have additional symptoms that suggest inattention to the space and/ or the body parts on the affected side or perception of a distorted body schema. (Body schema or body image is one's awareness of his *whole* body and its relationship to objects in the surrounding environment). These phenomena include anosognosia for hemiplegia, anosodiaphoria, allesthesia and allocusis, kinaesthetic hallucinations (i.e. imaginary limb movements), supernumerary (phantom) limbs and sensory extinction.

Anosognosia for hemiplegia

Anosognosia for hemiplegia is the patient's denial of the effects of stroke on his ability to perform motor tasks with the paralysed limbs. The patient will insist that his paralysed limb is functioning normally. In rare occasions a patient may claim that his hemiplegic limbs belong to someone else (personification anosognosia). Asomatognosia or depersonalisation, i.e. the patient's belief that part (usually half) of his body is missing, may also be present. Anosognosia was found in 17% of stroke patient in a population-based survey. A higher incidence of anosognosia for hemiplegia appears to be associated with large lesions in the deep white matter of the right parietal lobe and the basal ganglia. An association between a high incidence of anosognosia and the existence of a pre-stroke cognitive impairment has also been reported.

Anosodiaphoria

Anosodiaphoria is also common and is characterised by the patient's partial or complete lack of concern and indifference to the effects of the stroke, although the patient usually acknowledge the presence of limb weakness or skin sensory loss. Anosodiaphoria often occurs in patients without clinically obvious mood disorders.

Phantom limb phenomena

Although the presence of a phantom limb is frequently reported after limb amputations, occasionally patients with hemispatial neglect believe that they have one or more of phantom (supernumerary) limbs. This condition, which is thought to be due to sensory deafferentation, is also known as pseudoploymelia. The patient is usually alert and has normal cognitive and psychological function. The phantom perception is vivid, recurrent and does not change over time. In some cases the phantom limb was reported to have been "attached" to the paralysed limb, while in other cases it was completely separate from the hemiplegic arm and leg. Anosognosia and anosodiaphoria may or may not be present.

Allesthesia
A tendency to mislocate tactile stimuli to the opposite (non-affected) side of the body when the affected side is stimulated is known as allesthesia. The term allocusis is used when the same phenomenon is caused by an auditory stimulus. Allesthesia and allocusis usually interfere with the patient's ability to interact with the surrounding environment. For example, in the presence of allocusis the patient may ignore the sounds that arise in the neglected hemispace and consequently fails to make the appropriate response to them.

Sensory extinction
In contrast to allesthesia and allocusis which can be readily diagnosed by observing the patient's behaviour, sensory extinction is found only on physical examination. The patient with extinction will perceive the stimulus normally if it is presented on either side of the body separately. However, if the same stimulus is presented on both sides simultaneously, it will be perceived only on the unaffected side. Extinction may involve any or all sensory modalities. The impact of extinction on the performance of activities of daily living (ADL) and on functional recovery is not clear. However, a better understanding of this phenomenon may be useful for developing treatment strategies, e.g. the use of unilateral cueing on the affected side.

Incidence of unilateral hemispatial neglect
The reports of the incidence and prevalence of post-stroke UHN are conflicting. According to different studies, the estimated incidence varies from less than 20% to more than 90%. This variation is probably due to the different criteria that were used to define UHN and the different assessment tools used for its diagnosis. The timing of the patients' assessment may have also been a factor, as spontaneous recovery of UHN occurs in the first few days after stroke in many patients. Consequently, more patients with UHN would be expected in the early stages after stroke with subsequent reduction in the numbers of affected individuals in the chronic phase of the disease.

Pathogenesis

Typically UHN results from lesions of the non-dominant (usually the right) parietal lobe. In most cases it is due to lesions in the inferior right parietal lobe or the right parieto-temporal junction. However, it is sometimes seen in patients with left hemisphere stroke. Other structures that may be associated with UHN are the deep white matter of the parietal lobe, the frontal lobe, the thalamus and the basal ganglia. UHN resulting from left hemisphere lesions is relatively rare and is usually mild. It also tends to recover faster and more completely.

The disparity in the frequency and severity of left and right UHN has been attributed to the differences in the functional specialisation of the two hemispheres. According to a hypothesis known as the orientational bias model of UHN, each hemisphere is capable of directing attention to the opposite side of space. However, because of functional asymmetry of the two hemispheres orientation is preferentially directed to the right hemispace. Normally attention to either the left or right hemispace is achieved by a process of reciprocal inhibition of the relevant hemisphere. Consequently, right-sided brain lesions result in attentional bias to the right (and left hemispatial neglect) because of the unopposed action of the left hemisphere. The opposite is also true, except that the orientational bias to the left is weaker. Therefore, lesions in the right parietal lobe cause UHN more frequently and result in more severe symptoms than left hemisphere lesions. UHN has also been attributed to impairment of sustained attention and to difficulties with the initiation of eye movements to the contralesional space.

Clinical features

UHN is frequently associated with hemiplegia. Although peripheral spinothalamic and proprioceptive sensation is usually intact, a visual field defect is often present. Sensory extinction and allesthesia can be easily demonstrated on neurological examination and allocusis and anosognosia for hemiplegia may be elicited by observing the patient's behaviour. The features of UHN are:

1. The main feature of UHN is the patient's apparent failure to spontaneously explore the extrapersonal space or to direct attention or to respond to stimuli in the hemispace opposite to the side of the brain lesion. The neglect may involve a body part, or stimuli in the peripersonal space (i.e. space that is within the subject's reach) or far space. A patient with severe UHN is

unaware of events on the affected hemispace. Typically, he does not respond to sounds arising in the neglected hemispace or acknowledge the presence of people on that side. The hemiplegic arm often dangles limply by the side of the bed or chair and when the paralysed leg is caught under the wheelchair the patient does not show any awareness of this or concern about the potential harm that this may cause.

2. Usually the further the location of the object or the stimulus in the neglected hemispace from the patient's body mid line, the more likely that it will be ignored. Interestingly, UHN is sometimes observed for the left half of an object irrespective of its location in relation to other objects in the hemispace. This is known as object-based neglect. Frequently the patient may demonstrate neglect behaviour for one stimulus but responds appropriately to another. For example, he may respond to sounds coming from the neglected hemispace but fails to notice food in the left side of the plate.

3. Lack of insight into the impairments or their functional consequences is a characteristic feature of severe UHN. As a result, the patients often rationalise or play down their difficulties or even deny the existence of such difficulties.

4. The patient usually does not attempt to compensate for the UHN, for example by visual scanning to search the environment on the affected side. In fact, patients with severe UHN frequently turn their heads away from the neglected extrapersonal space.

5. A patient with relatively preserved motor and sensory function in the affected upper limb (usually the left arm) may not use it for functional tasks. This is known as motor neglect. Typically motor neglect does not affect automatic actions, such as arm swing during walking.

6. Patients with UHN may also have neglect dyslexia and neglect dysgraphia. Neglect dyslexia manifests as omission, addition or substitution of the first letter when reading single words. For instance, 'reel' is read 'eel' or 'fed' becomes 'bed'. On the other hand, when reading a text, the patient may ignore the first few words of each line and starts reading from the middle (i.e. the right half) of the page. Writing is affected in a similar way. Patients with neglect dysgraphia typically omit the first letter when writing single words or squeeze all of the text on the right side of the page when they write a paragraph.

7. Neglect behaviour increases, or may even appear for the first time, when the patient is tired or during an intercurrent illness, such as a urinary tract or chest infection.

Differential diagnosis –
UHN is often confused with homonymous hemianopia. Although both of these impairments may be present in the same patient, it is important to distinguish between the two. This distinction provides valuable prognostic information on the potential for functional recovery and is useful for planning the therapeutic interventions. It is usually possible to make the correct differential diagnosis on the basis of clinical observations alone, as shown in the table below. However, formal mapping of the visual fields with perimetry may sometimes be necessary.

Table 3.5
Comparison between the clinical features of unilateral hemispatial neglect (UHN) and hemianopia

Clinical feature	Hemianopia	UHN
Insight into disability	Intact	Poor
Compensatory head movements	Present	Absent
Spontaneous searching eye saccades	Present	Absent or weak
Observation during activities of daily living	No neglect behaviour	Evidence of neglect behaviour
Use of compensatory strategies in functional tasks	Yes	No

Diagnostic tests for unilateral hemispatial neglect –
Numerous tests have been used for the diagnosis of UHN. Observation of the patient's spontaneous behaviour and his response to external stimuli often provides sufficient evidence for the presence or absence of UHN. Further evidence may be

obtained from the patient's performance on bedside tests. These tests fall into four main groups, namely drawing from memory, copying, line bisection and cancellation tasks. There are different variations of each of these tests.

The line bisection test is the simplest of these tests. The patient is required to mark the middle of a single 28 cm long horizontal line drawn on an A4 paper. The paper is placed in front of the patient so that it corresponds to the middle of the body. The test result is scored by measuring the deviation of the patient's mark from the true line centre. Cancellation tasks are also frequently used. Of these tasks, the star cancellation test is claimed to be the most reliable. In this task the patient is asked to cross out the small stars on a drawing consisting 52 large stars and 13 letters of the English alphabet that are randomly positioned among 54 small stars (27 on each half of the page). UHN is diagnosed when the patient fails to cross out all the small stars in the relevant half of the page. If targets are missed on both sides then it is likely that the patient has a deficit of generalised attention or object-centered neglect, rather than lateralized unilateral hemispatial neglect.

The results of bedside tests should be interpreted with caution. Some patients show evidence of neglect on some of these tests but not on others. For example, a patient may copy a drawing correctly and yet fails to complete the star cancellation task successfully (see figure 3.1). In addition, performance on the bedside tests appears to be affected by the subject's age and other factors, such as fatigue. Healthy older people with no clinically demonstrable evidence of neurological or other disease may omit many targets on the star cancellation task. For this reason the use of a test battery or a combination of some of these tests with standardised behavioural observations may provide a more comprehensive assessment. It has been reported that about three quarters of cases of UHN can be detected when the line biscetion task and the star cancellation test are used together. A more comprehensive assessment scale is the Behavioural Inattention Test (BIT). This assessment scale is made of 15 items including pen-and-paper tests and behavioural tests. The BIT is particularly useful, as the scores on this test seem to correlate with the patient's performance in ADL.

The line bisection test appears to be useful for the initial screening for hemispatial neglect, whereas the BIT is more appropriate for in-depth assessment and is usually used in research.

Figure 3.1

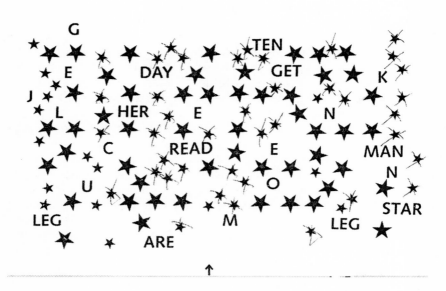

Performance of a patient with a hemispatial neglect on three tests.

The functional consequences of unilateral hemispatial neglect

It is not difficult to appreciate the impact of severe, persistent UHN on the subject's functional abilities and the potential for social participation. UHN causes difficulties with safe mobility (e.g. turning over in bed, transfers from bed to chair, walking), activities of daily living, reading and writing, leisure activities and employment. It also reduces the effectiveness of rehabilitation by interfering with learning of new motor skills and by preventing the use of strategies to compensate for the functional deficits. Patients with UHN often do not have insight into their difficulties and fail to appreciate the need to engage in rehabilitative interventions. Understandably, a patient with poor insight into his disability is unlikely to cooperate with therapy and may even consider the treatment unnecessary. Patients with UHN usually also have a longer stay in hospital compared to other stroke patients and are often less independent at home after discharge.

Treatment

UHN contributes significantly to the functional disability after stroke. Yet at present there are no therapeutic interventions that have been conclusively shown to ameliorate this deficit or to significantly enhance the patient's ability to compensate for it and, thus, improve the functional outcomes. This is despite the research evidence of improvement in the patients' scores on impairment-based outcome measures. Generally, four therapeutic strategies have been used in the rehabilitation of patients with UHN. These are:

1. *Methods that attempt to compensate for the symptoms of UHN*

These are known as impairment training or transfer of training. They are based on the use of visual, tactile or auditory cues to encourage the patient to scan and explore the neglected hemispace. These strategies often improve performance in reading and writing tasks but usually do not generalise to other activities or result in more functional independence.

2. *Methods that enhance the patient's awareness of the UHN*

These methods consist of task-specific training. The patient is prompted to direct and maintain his attention to the affected hemispace and is reminded with an alerting device, e.g. a flashing light or bell ringing, when his attention falters. Task-specific (spatio-motor or functional) training is based on the assumption that frequent practice of a given functional skill, e.g. dressing oneself, will result in learning and more functional independence. Strategies that improve general attention and arousal and exploit the patient's voluntary attentional mechanisms (such as feedback) also tend to reduce UHN.

3. *Methods that orientate the neglected hemispace to the patient's reference frame.*
These include the use of eye patches to cover the visual field ipsilateral to the brain lesion and the use of Fresnel prisims (which can be orientated to displace the retinal image to the left or right as required). Similarly, caloric stimulation of the brain stem vestibular system through the irrigation of the ipsilateral ear with ice-cold water or by inducing optokinetic nystagmus also reduces UHN. However, the effect of the latter interventions is usually transient and has no enduring clinical benefit.

4. *The use of dopamine agonists for the treatment of UHN*
It has been claimed that dopamine agonists promote recovery from UHN due to a specific effect on the neural circuits concerned with the exploration of space. However, a non-specific arousal or a motivational effect are also possible. Bromocriptine in a dose of 15 mg daily for 3-4 weeks was reported to have improved the symptoms of chronic UHN. A similar, but transient effect was also observed after a single injection of apomorphine (2 mg). The reported beneficial effect of these drugs on UHN was based on few single case studies and has not yet been evaluated in large scale randomised controlled trials. On the whole, to date drug treatment of UHN has not received wide acceptance by clinicians.

Prognosis
Right-sided UHN has a better prognosis than neglect of the left hemispace. Patients with right neglect improve faster and their recovery is usually more complete. Recovery is usually faster in the first 10 days than at any subsequent stage of stroke. It is often complete in most patients in 3 months. Persistence of UHN for more than three months after stroke is uncommon, and has been estimated to occur in about 10% of cases. It is usually associated with extensive hemisphere damage and/ or involvement of subcortical structures and with the presence of anosognosia for hemiplegia in the first 2-3 days of the stroke. Object-based neglect is thought to have a worse prognosis than body-centred neglect. It tends to persist for longer periods and

is more difficult to treat than body-centred neglect. Occasionally UHN was found several years after the cerebrovascular event. Persistent, severe UHN is probably the strongest predictor of poor functional independence after stroke.

IMPAIRMENTS OF VISUAL FUNCTION

Most stroke patients report visual symptoms in the acute phase of the disease and in some cases these symptoms persist for months or years. The nature of the visual disturbances depends largely on the site and size of the brain lesion. Partial visual field loss is common after anterior circulation stroke and is due to damage to the fibres of the optic tract or corona radiata (in the posterior limb of the internal capsule or temporo-occipital lobe, respectively). By contrast, involvement of the occipital cortex or the parieto-occipital area usually causes disturbances of visual perception, while patients with brain stem stroke often complain of double vision.

The typical visual field loss after stroke in the territory of the middle cerebral artery is a homonymous hemianopia or a homonymous quadrantanopia. The patient usually has insight into the visual deficit and often reports difficulties with reading (hemianopic dyslexia) and/ or partial blindness. Hemianopia should not be confused with unilateral hemispatial neglect, although the two may co-exist. As described earlier, the distinction between these conditions can often be made on clinical examination alone (see the section on unilateral hemispatial neglect). Homonymous hemianopia can be easily confirmed on the bedside assessment of the visual fields using the confrontation method, but sometimes a formal assessment with perimetry may be necessary. The confrontation method of visual fields assessment is based on comparing the patient's fields with those of the examiner. (It assumes that the examiner has normal visual fields).

Rarely, patients with occipital lobe stroke and intact eyesight may experience difficulties with recognizing familiar faces (prosopognosia), naming colours in the absence of colour blindness and aphasia (colour agnosia) or identifying objects by only looking at them (visual object agnosia). The agnosia is related only to the visual modality and face and object recognition are possible through other sensory modalities, i.e. smell, touch and sound.

Although the post-stroke visual impairments often recover spontaneously, in some patients the deficits become permanent. Rehabilitation of patients with visual field loss should aim to restore vision or, if this is not possible, to improve the residual visual function. It should also include training programmes that enhance the functional ability of the visually impaired individual in vision-related tasks in different environmental conditions and different times of the day. Different methods of treatment may be used individually or in combination. These include visual restitution training with or without attentional cueing, compensatory visual field scanning, manipulation of light conditions and the use of optical devices, such as prisms that relocate the image to the intact area of the visual field. Occlusion of one eye (with an eye patch or a covered spectacle lens) is often sufficient for the successful management of diplopia, but surgery may be required in chronic, severe cases.

MOTOR SYSTEM DISORDERS

Muscle weakness of the upper motor neurone type resulting in hemiplegia is the commonest motor disorder after stroke. Extrapyramidal system syndromes, including 'vascular' parkinsonism, gait and balance disturbances and various involuntary movements, may also occur.

MUSCLE WEAKNESS
Most stroke patients present with unilateral muscle weakness of varying severity. In the acute phase the muscle tone is also reduced in all but the mildest of cases. The result is flaccid hemiplegia or hemiparesis. Usually the motor disability is compounded by other impairments, such as poor balance, proprioceptive sensory loss, unilateral hemispatial neglect or a hemianopic visual field defect. Frequently, the muscle weakness is not only confined to the hemiplegic side. Subtle weakness of the "good" limbs is usually present in the first week of the cerebrovascular event. (A small percentage of pyramidal tract fibres descends uncrossed and innervates muscles of the ipsilateral limbs). The severity of muscle weakness ipsilateral to the brain lesion is usually proportional to the severity of the stroke.

Muscle weakness following hemiplegic stroke often leads to a wide range of disabilities. Involvement of facial muscles may lead to dysarthria and dysphagia. Weakness of the upper limb may render the hand functionally useless. In the early phase of stroke patients are usually unable to maintain an independent sitting balance due to weakness of trunk muscles and postural instability. The ability to change one's position in bed (bed mobility) and to transfer from bed to chair etc is also lost or severely reduced. Even when recovery occurs, the patient's gait and posture are seldom fully restored.

Assessment
A baseline measurement of the severity of muscle weakness that is followed by serial assessments is essential for planning therapy and for the evaluation of the response to therapeutic interventions. It also provides valuable prognostic information as the severity of the initial motor impairment usually correlates with the degree of functional recovery after stroke, especially in mobility and some activities of daily living (ADL). In clinical practice muscle strength is assessed by observing the posture and voluntary movements of the affected limb and by comparing the patient's muscle strength with that of the examiner. The scale of the Medical Research Council (MRC), which has the advantage of being simple and brief, may be used to record the degree of muscle weakness (table 3.6). Other scales, such as the Motricity Index, are time-consuming and are more suitable for research. (For a detailed description of the Motricity Index see Demeurisse et al, 1980).

Table 3.6 – The MRC scale

Grade	Description
0	No voluntary movement
1	Flicker of a movement
2	Movement present, but only if the effect of gravity is removed
3	Movement present against gravity, but not against the examiner's resistance to movement
4	Movement present against gravity and resistance, but weaker than normal
5	Full muscle strength (allowing for the patient's age & body built)

There is no linear correlation between the increase in muscle strength, as measured with the MRC scale, and the improvement in motor functional abilities. Therefore, the additional use of functional assessment tools provides important prognostic information and also helps with planning the therapy programme. The most valuable of these in routine clinical practice is the regular assessment of sitting and standing balance.

Assessment of the patient's static and dynamic sitting balance is important in the early stage of stroke because good sitting balance is an essential prerequisite for being able to transfer from one place to another, to stand or to walk. Static sitting balance may be defined as the patient's ability to sit still without holding on to an object and without assistance from others or additional external support, such as being propped up by pillows. Most stroke patients regain static sitting balance in about 3 or 4 weeks after the acute cerebro-vascular event. In another 2 to 3 weeks they would also be expected to have a dynamic sitting balance. Recovery of dynamic sitting balance will enable the patient to maintain a safe unsupported sitting posture, even when the sitting balance is challenged, e.g. while reaching for far objects.

It is usually sufficient to assess the sitting balance by carefully observing the patient during unsupported sitting and during activities that cause perturbation of balance, e.g. raising the unaffected arm, throwing objects or reaching for objects that are placed beyond arm's length. Similarly, assessment of standing balance can be made by the clinical observation of postural sway and the symmetry of the distribution of body weight on both legs during standing.

Management
There is no specific treatment that reverses muscle paralysis. Natural recovery of motor function occurs in the vast majority of patients, but the extent of improvement and the speed with which it occurs vary widely between individuals. The aim of management is to prevent complications, to enhance biological recovery and to help the patient learn new strategies to compensate for the motor disability. The development of muscle spasticity, shoulder subluxation and injury, e.g. ankle joint damage due to proprioceptive sensory loss or unilateral hemispatial neglect, are common but preventable complications in patients with motor weakness.

Muscle spasticity tends to develop soon after the initial phase of flaccid paralysis, especially in patients with intracerebral haemorrhage. It may cause further functional disability, pain and muscle spasms. Spasticity also predisposes to the development of fixed muscle contractures (see chapter four). The prevention and prompt treatment of these complications is, therefore, of paramount importance. To this end, meticulous attention should be paid to the correct positioning of the hemiplegic patient while lying in bed, rolling over in bed and during transfers from bed to chair, and during sitting and standing. The optimal posture is that the shoulder on the hemiplegic side is maintained in a protracted, i.e. a forward, position. The arm is slightly externally rotated and extended at the elbow and wrist. The hip should also be protracted but internally rotated. When the patient is lying in bed the same posture should be adopted and, in addition, the knee on the hemiplegic side should also be slightly flexed. The same principles should be followed when bridging is attempted, e.g. in order to use a bedpan. (Bridging is lifting the pelvis off the bed whilst lying prone with the hips and knees flexed).

The cornerstone of the management of patients with motor weakness is physical therapy. It has been shown to enhance neural plasticity, especially if it is started early. Different physiotherapy methods are used, including the Bobath neuro-developmental technique, proprioceptive neuromuscular facilitation and the motor relearning programme (MLP). In Britain the Bobath method is the most widely used form of physiotherapy intervention. This method is based on the premise that upper motor neurone lesions cause spasticity by releasing abnormal postural reflexes from cortical control. It is suggested that the resulting hypertonus leads to poor static postures that interfere with dynamic postural control and functional movements. Consequently, the Bobath technique focuses on suppression of the abnormal postural patterns of flexor and extensor spasticity while encouraging movement patterns that facilitate normal motor activities. The emphasis of this method of treatment is on improving dynamic postures and on encouraging selective movement patterns by breaking down the motor task into its constituent parts. For example, the therapist may support the elbow of the paretic upper limb (inhibition of abnormal postures through proximal fixation) so that the patient is able to use his hand (facilitation of normal, selective movements).

The proprioceptive neuromuscular facilitation physiotherapy approach utilizes the use of sensory stimulation to improve motor function. By contrast, the motor learning programme (MLP) is based on task and context specific functional training, the management of muscle tone and muscle strengthening exercises. It is delivered through a process of goal setting, instructions and feedback.

There is no convincing evidence that any of the above-mentioned physiotherapy methods is superior to the others in terms of motor recovery or better functional gains in activities of daily living. However, interventions that are based on repetitive training practice in specific functional motor tasks, such as MLP, appear to result in faster functional improvement and shorter hospital stay. In practice, usually different aspects of these methods are used together.

The frequency and duration of physiotherapy sessions that produce the optimal motor functional recovery after stroke have not been established. It is not surprising therefore, that in practice the intensity of therapy is often determined by the patient's tolerance of the intervention and the available therapy resources. The balance of the currently available evidence, however, suggests a correlation between treatment intensity and functional outcomes in some cases. For example, intensive therapy (defined here as 15 hours/ week) has been shown to be beneficial in patients with upper limb weakness in the presence of residual voluntary movements of the paretic hand, but not when there is complete motor weakness.

Apart from conventional physiotherapy several other therapeutic modalities have been introduced for the treatment of motor weakness in recent years. These include constraint-induced therapy, treadmill training, biofeedback, functional electrical stimulation and the use of robotic devices. At present there is no conclusive evidence of the effectiveness of these methods.

Course and prognosis
Motor recovery usually follows a predictable pattern that is independent of the type of stroke. It usually starts in the proximal muscles groups. Distal muscles, especially muscles of the upper limb, tend to recover last, if at all. Most of the functional gains occur in the first three months after stroke. A combination of motor recovery and muscle hypertonia enables more than 80% of stroke survivors to walk again. However, recovery of upper

limb function is generally poor and nearly all patients with a dense hemiplegia never regain full functional use of the affected hand.

LIMB AND TRUNK ATAXIA

Ataxia is a disorder of the execution of goal-directed voluntary movements in the absence of significant muscle weakness, severe abnormality of muscle tone, dyspraxia and involuntary movements of the affected limbs. Ataxia in stroke may result from direct damage to the cerebellum (cerebellar ataxia) or from impairment or loss of proprioception (sensory ataxia), e.g. following thalamic stroke.

Mild limb ataxia is usually asymptomatic and is detected on clinical examination with the finger-nose test and the heel-shin test. As a rule, it has no effect on motor function. In moderately severe ataxia the motor activity is carried out in a clumsy, uncoordinated way. The trajectory of the limb movement is inaccurate but the intended motor task is frequently accomplished, albeit with difficulty. By contrast, in severe ataxia the limb frequently misses the target and the patient is unable to use the limb effectively. Trunk ataxia results in difficulties with sitting unsupported, and with walking.

Ataxia may interfere with the patient's mobility and activities of daily living, including feeding, and personal care. Different methods are used for the management of ataxia. The main therapeutic intervention consists of stabilization of the proximal limb segment combined with balance training and visual feedback. Other treatment strategies are less effective and include the use of wrist weights to reduce upper limb excursion (in order to control the range and direction of movement) and the prescription of drugs, such as isoniazid (900-1200 mg/day), primidone (250-750 mg/day) and propranolol (40-120 mg/day).

VASCULAR EXTRAPYRAMIDAL SYNDROMES

Stroke may cause almost any involuntary movement. It may also abolish a pre-existing involuntary movement, for example hand tremor. The involuntary movements usually occur in the early post-stroke period, but in some patients their onset is delayed by months or even years. Post-stroke movement disorders usually result from lesions in the basal ganglia, thalamus or cerebral cortex. However, there is no strong correlation between the site of the cerebral infarct or haemorrhage and a given extrapyramidal syndrome. The commonest movement disorders after stroke

93

are parkinsonism, dystonia, chorea and hemiballismus (sudden, violent involuntary movement arising at a proximal joint of the arm or leg). Sometimes patients develop other difficulties with walking, such as ataxic or shuffling gait. By contrast, a few patients with an otherwise normal gait become unable to initiate stepping at the beginning of walking or on turning around (the syndrome of gait ignition failure).

Vascular parkinsonism is thought to occur in about 2% of stroke patients. It is usually seen in those with a history of diabetes and/ or hypertension and recurrent strokes. Vascular parkinsonism is usually associated with cerebral small vessel disease and lacunar infarcts. It can be distinguished from idiopathic parkinsonism by the additional finding of pyramidal tract signs on clinical examination, the usual absence of tremor and the frequent co-existence of cognitive impairment or frank dementia. In addition, as a rule vascular parkinsonism does not respond well to optimal doses of dopaminergic drugs.

BLADDER AND BOWEL DYSFUNCTION

URINARY INCONTINENCE
Incontinence of urine that occurs *de novo* in the first 24 hours after stroke is relatively common and has been shown to be a poor prognostic sign both for the patient's survival in the early phase of stroke and for functional recovery. One in two patients with no history of urinary incontinence or an intercurrent urinary tract infection (UTI) will be expected to lose control over their bladder function after stroke. Six months after stroke 20% of those who survive still remain incontinent. Incontinence is more common after stroke in the territory of the anterior cerebral artery and its incidence appears to correlate with the infarct size. For example, a patient with a lesion involving cortical and subcortical structures is five times more likely to become incontinent than one with a purely cortical or purely subcortical infarct. In addition to the infarct size, severe initial functional disability, dysphasia and cognitive impairment are also strong predictors of post-stroke urinary incontinence.

Long-term incontinence of urine usually has a profound effect on the patient's morale and self-esteem. Furthermore, by interfering with one's ability to maintain adequate personal hygiene, it may prevent return to gainful employment, and may also reduce opportunities for socialisation and outdoor leisure activities. Urinary retention as a direct result of stroke is less common and is usually due to bladder neck obstruction or the use of anticholinergic and other drugs.

Differential diagnosis
The causes and the underlying mechanisms of urinary incontinence in stroke patients are diverse and include neurological and non-neurological disorders. The direct damage to neural structures due to stroke may result in loss of the supraspinal control of bladder function. In some cases urinary incontinence may be due to coincidental prostatic disease, stress incontinence, UTI, reduced consciousness or cognitive impairment. It is important to establish the cause of incontinence because effective management almost invariably depends on making the correct diagnosis.

Stroke causes urinary incontinence by interrupting the neural pathways that control bladder function. The initiation of micturition and the maintenance of continence are regulated by a group of neurones in the medial aspect of the frontal lobes. The axons of these cells descend through the internal capsule to the brain stem, terminating mainly in the pontine reticular formation. Fibres from the brain stem nuclei continue as part of the spinoreticular, and medial and anterior reticulospinal tracts. The first two tracts convey neural impulses that initiate micturition. They facilitate contraction of the detrusor muscle and relaxation of the urethral sphincter. The function of the anterior reticulospinal tract is to promote continence by inhibiting the detrusor muscle and by causing the urethral sphincter to contract. Damage to the corticospinal pathways often leads to involuntary contractions of the detrusor muscle during bladder filling. This is known as detrusor hyper-reflexia and is the main type of incontinence that occurs as a direct result of stroke. Detrusor hyper-reflexia has been reported in more than a third of patients in the first three months after the cerebro-vascular event. It is seen even more frequently in the chronic stages of stroke.

Bladder dysfunction similar to that of detrusor hyper-reflexia may also be present in elderly subjects in the absence of neurological disease. This is often referred to as detrusor muscle instability. Typically, the patient with detrusor muscle hyper-reflexia or instability experiences urinary frequency and urge incontinence. Nocturnal enuresis may also occur.

About 20% of stroke patients have dertusor hypo-reflexia. This form of incontinence is usually caused by damage to the sacral nerve roots. When it occurs in stroke patients it is often due to coincidental diabetic autonomic neuropathy. It may also result from treatment with anticholinergic drugs. The characteristic feature of detrusor hypo-reflexia is an overdistended bladder with increased capacity (700 ml or more) and overflow incontinence.

In a small number of stroke patients the detrusor muscle contraction is not accompanied by the coordinated relaxation of the urethral sphincter, a condition known as detrusor-sphincter dyssynergia (DSD). This results in reflux of urine into the ureters and, if the condition is not recognised and treated early, may lead to hydronephrosis and renal failure. DSD is common in patients with spinal cord lesions but has occasionally been reported after stroke of the dorsolateral part of the pons or basal ganglia. Clinically, the symptoms of DSD are similar to those of detrusor hyper-reflexia, except that difficulties with voiding are also present. Videourodynamic studies are invaluable for distinguishing between these two conditions.

Bladder neck obstruction due to benign prostatic hypertrophy is a common cause of overflow incontinence in middle aged and elderly men. Constipation, faecal impaction and the use of anticholinergic drugs or diuretics may trigger this form of incontinence or precipitate urinary retention. The patient usually gives a history of difficulties with micturition and a weak stream of urine preceding the onset of incontinence (or retention) by several months or even years. Because bladder emptying is incomplete dribbling of urine between acts of voiding is a common and characteristic symptom.

Stress incontinence is frequently reported by females after middle age and is especially common in multiparous women. This form of incontinence is thought to occur partly because the female urethra is short and wide and does not possess an internal urethral sphincter. Weakness of the muscles of the pelvic floor may also cause descent of the bladder neck and lead to incompetence of the external urethral sphincter. The hallmark of this form of incontinence is that leakage of urine is triggered by actions that raise the intra-abdominal pressure, e.g. coughing, sneezing or laughing. The table below summarises the main features of the different types of urinary incontinence.

Table 3.7
The differential diagnosis of urinary incontinence

Type of incontinence	Urgency	Difficult voiding	Fre-quency	Nocturia	Enuresis
Detru-sor hyper-reflexia	+++	0	+++	++	++
Stress inconti-nence	0	0	0/+	0	0
Over-flow inconti-nence	0	++	Drib-bling	+	+
UTI	++	0/+ (dys-uria)	+++	+	+
Demen-tia etc	0	0	0	++	+
DSD	++	++	++	++	+

0 = absent, + = mild, ++ = moderate, +++ = severe

Assessment
A carefully taken micturitional history followed by abdominal and rectal examination is the cornerstone of diagnosis of bladder dysfunction. Not only does it help with identifying the cause of incontinence, but it should also identify the impact of this symptom on the individual and provide useful information for the choice of the best possible treatment strategy.

Irritative symptoms, such as frequency, urgency and nocturia, are characteristic of DSD and detrusor instability. However, the combination of these symptoms with dysuria usually indicates the presence of an uncomplicated UTI. If loin pain, fever and chills are also present, a diagnosis of pyelonephritis must be given serious consideration. The obstructive urinary symptoms are voiding difficulty, urinary hesitancy and weak stream of urine. These symptoms suggest bladder neck obstruction which is commonly caused by benign prostatic hypertrophy.

It is important to obtain a baseline assessment of the severity of incontinence in order to monitor the response to therapeutic interventions. A simple assessment tool that was originally introduced for epidemiological surveys of urinary incontinence may be used for this purpose (For more a detailed account see reference: Sandvik et al, 1993). It measures the frequency of incontinence on a five-point scale (0-4) and the amount leaked each time on a two-point scale as shown below in table 3.8. The score indicating the severity of incontinence is calculated by multiplying the scores of the two subsets. Scores of 1-2 and 3-4 indicate mild or moderately severe incontinence, respectively. The score of patients with severe incontinence ranges from 6 to 8.

Table 3.8
The severity of incontinence index

Subset A		Subset B	
Frequency of incontinence	Score	Amount of urine leaked	Score
Never	0	Drops/ little	1
<1 per month	1	More than a few drops	2
>1 per month	2		
1 or > per week	3		
Every day	4		

Initial screening of patients with bladder dysfunction should include urine microscopy and culture. A meticulous technique of urine collection and storage are essential to minimise the risk of bacterial contamination. Collection of the urine specimen must be done with the utmost care. As a rule, a mid stream urine is sufficient. When there is a urinary catheter in situ the urine sample should be collected by aspiration with a needle not by disconnecting the catheter from the bag. The urine should be examined within 4 hours of collection or should be stored at 4°C to avoid bacterial contamination. Asymptomatic bacteriuria is common and a diagnosis of UTI is made only if certain criteria are met. These are the presence of the typical symptoms, a bacterial count in excess of 10^4 colony-forming units per ml and a urine white cell count more than 10^3/ml.

In patients with obstructive urinary symptoms a bladder ultrasound scan is a useful non-invasive method for measuring the post-voiding residual volume. Intravenous urography may be necessary to demonstrate the presence or confirm the absence of dilatation of the ureters and the pelvicalyceal renal system. Evaluation of the renal function and the measurement of serum electrolytes are also an essential part of the patient's initial screening and subsequent monitoring.

In most cases sound treatment decisions can be made on the basis of the information derived from the above assessment. However, specialist investigations, such as videourodynamic studies, are sometimes required to distinguish between the different types of urinary incontinence.

Videourodynamic studies are helpful when it is difficult to distinguish on clinical grounds alone between detrusor hyper-reflexia and DSD. They are also indicated in incontinent patients with a history of pelvic surgery and in those presenting with a combination of symptoms that suggest an obstructive uropathy and neurogenic bladder dysfunction.

The interpretation of urodynamic studies
Healthy subjects normally experience a sensation of bladder filling before 300 ml of fluid are instilled in the bladder. Although spontaneous contractions of the detrusor muscle may be seen during bladder filling with volumes of up to 300 ml, these are weak and do not exceed 15 mm/H_2O. However, during voiding the contractions of the detrusor muscle increase in frequency and amplitude and are coordinated with the relaxation of the urethral sphincter. Neurogenic bladder dysfunction may interfere with the normal sensation of bladder filling, contractions of the derusor

muscle and the coordinated action of the latter with the urethral sphincter. For example, the threshold of bladder sensation is typically reduced in patients with detrusor hyper-reflexia and DSD and is increased when detrusor hyporeflexia is present. In the latter condition detrusor contractions are weak or absent with bladder volumes that would normally trigger bladder evacuation. A summary of the videourodynamic abnormalities associated with the different types of neurogenic bladder dysfunction is given in table 3.9.

Table 3.9
The main findings of videourodynamic studies in neurogenic bladder dysfunction

Mechanism of inconti- nence	Threshold of bladder sensation (in ml)	Detrusor contractions >15 mm H_2O at blad- der volume <300 ml	Sphincter during void- ing
Detrusor hy- per-reflexia	<300	Present	Relaxed
DSD	<300	Present	Contracted
Hyporeflexia	>450	Absent	Relaxed

Treatment
There are two main goals of treatment of neurogenic bladder dysfunction, irrespective of the underlying cause or the mechanism of incontinence. The first aim is to protect renal function and the second is to promote continence. The main measures that help to preserve renal function are the prevention and prompt treatment of UTI and ureteric reflux.

UTI is an important cause of morbidity and mortality in patients with neurogenic bladder dysfunction. Adequate fluid intake should be encouraged in order to reduce the risk of infection. In most cases UTI is due to E. coli infection and it usually responds to a 5-7 day course of trimethoprim. Second line drugs include cephalexin and nitrofurantoin. Levofloxacin (250 mg qds for 10 days) is the drug of choice in cases of pyelonephritis. Infections with proteus species must be eradicated as they predispose to the formation of bladder calculi. Acidification of urine by drinking fruit juices (for example cranberry juice) or with orally administered ascorbic acid tablets is a useful strategy for preventing recurrent UTI. However, the use of a urinary antiseptic, such as hexamine, may be necessary in resistant cases or chronic bacteruria. The long-term prophylactic use of antibacterial drugs is not recommended except in the presence of recurrent UTI and renal impairment. Similarly, asymptomatic bacterial colonisation of urinary catheters is common and does not require treatment with antibacterial drugs.

Intermittent self-catheterisation (ISC) is a useful management strategy in patients with neurogenic bladder dysfunction, especially in the presence of chronic or recurrent UTI. ISC has been shown to reduce the frequency of UTI if it is performed at least 4 times a day and the urine volume is kept below 400 ml between catheterisations. The procedure is safe and acceptable to most patients. Urethral stricture (as a result of repeated trauma) is a rare complication, especially if low friction catheters are used. Patients with bladder neck obstruction may require surgical treatment, for example resection of a hypertrophied prostate or a sphincterotomy for DSD. Surgery for bladder neck obstruction safeguards against ureteric reflux and renal damage.

Promotion of urinary continence
It might be necessary to recommend an indwelling urinary catheter for the first few days or even weeks after stroke to reduce the risk of skin pressure sores developing in patients with severely impaired mobility or in those with a low level of consciousness. Catheterisation at this stage also has the additional advantage of allowing uninterrupted sleep at night which reduces day time fatigue. It also reduces the burden of nursing care. However, removal of the catheter should be considered once the patient has regained sufficient mobility and alertness and is able to use a bedpan or to transfer onto a commode safely (with or without assistance).

Bed wetting during sleep may be reduced by advising the patient to restrict his fluid intake to 1.5 litres/ 24 hours, to take the last drink in late afternoon and to avoid drinking tea and coffee (caffeine has a diuretic effect). Bladder training (scheduled voiding) is also an effective measure and is successful in about 50% of patients. The patient is asked to urinate initially every two hours with progressive lengthening of the periods between voiding until continence is re-established. When these measures fail continence may be achieved by the use of condom (penile sheath) drainage, incontinence pads, a dribble pouch or other similar devices. Long-term catheterisation should be considered a last resort in the management of urinary incontinence. Silicon catheters are preferable to latex catheters and can be left in situ for 6-8 weeks.

Drug treatment of urinary incontinence
Antimuscarinic drugs, such as oxybutanin and tolterodine, inhibit the activity of the detrusor muscle and are frequently used in the treatment of detrusor hyper-reflexia and detrusor instability. The two drugs have a comparable efficacy and exert their maximal effect several weeks after the commencement of therapy. Antimuscarinic drugs are effective in about 60% of cases and long-term treatment is often necessary as the symptoms may relapse when the drug is discontinued. Anticholinergic adverse effects are common, especially if the optimal drug dose is prescribed from the outset. To reduce the possibility of drug adverse effects it is recommended that treatment with oxybutanin is started in a dose of 2.5 mg once a day. The dose is then titrated up in increments of 2.5 mg every 3-4 days until the patient is continent or to a maximum dose of 5 mg tds. The slow release version of oxybutanin is as effective and is better tolerated than the standard preparation. Tolterodine 2 mg bd is an alternative to oxybutanin.

BOWEL DYSFUNCTION
About 40% of patients develop faecal incontinence in the acute phase of stroke and most of these patients will also have urinary incontinence. Of those who survive 10% will continue to be incontinent of faeces in the long-term. (This contrasts with a prevalence of faecal incontinence of approximately 2% in the general adult population). Post-stroke faecal incontinence occurs more often in elderly frail patients, especially females. Its incidence also increases with the severity of stroke and in diabetics.

Differential diagnosis
The control of defecation depends on the normal functioning of the frontal lobe and the corticospinal tracts. In addition, the anatomical and functional integrity of the internal anal sphincter, the puborectalis muscle and external anal sphincter are also

essential for continence. Consequently, a large number of pathological conditions can potentially cause faecal incontinence, as shown below. (See table 3.10).

Table 3.10
The main causes of faecal incontinence in stroke patients

Cause of faecal incontinence	Mechanism
Lesion in frontal lobe or pyramidal tracts	Loss of cortical control
S2-S4 root lesion (e.g. diabetic neuropathy)	Reduced or absent rectal sensation
Faecal impaction, laxative abuse	Reduced rectal storage capacity
Old age, surgery, obstetric complications	Incompetent anal sphincter
Cognitive impairment, mental illness	Poor social awareness

Faecal incontinence as a direct result of stroke usually occurs with frontal lobe infarcts. However, constipation, faecal impaction and overflow of soft stools are probably the commonest causes of faecal incontinence in the stroke population. Other causes include laxative abuse, immobility (especially if combined with severe communication difficulties due to dysphasia or dysarthria), cognitive impairment and coincidental surgical and obstetric disorders that compromise the integrity of the anal sphincter, such as rectal or vaginal prolapse.

Assessment
The evaluation of a faecally incontinent patient should include assessment of the severity of the incontinence and a diagnostic work-up of its underlying cause. The severity of faecal incontinence can be established from the history and physical examination. Severe faecal incontinence is characterised by frequent loss of bowel control irrespective of the consistency of the stools. By contrast, in cases of mild incontinence the patients soil their underpants with small amounts of loose or semi-formed stools. Mild incontinence should not be confused with soiling due to prolapsed haemarroids, an anal fistula or vaginal discharge.

A carefully taken history and clinical examination are often sufficient to elucidate the cause of faecal incontinence. For example, a previous history of anorectal surgery, obstetric complications and laxative abuse may provide useful clues to the cause of the faecal incontinence. Inspection of the perineum may confirm the presence of a rectal or vaginal prolapse or scarring from a previous episiotomy. An absent ano-cutaneous reflex suggests disruption of the sacral reflex arc due to a neuropathy or a cauda equina lesion. A lax anal sphincter on rectal examination would suggest incompetence of the anal sphincter and the presence of a large amount of hard faeces in the rectum is diagnostic of faecal impaction. Specialist investigations, such as anal manometry, endoanal ultrasound, anorectal electromyography and nerve conduction studies of the pudendal nerve may be needed, especially if surgical treatment is being considered.

Management

Treatment of faecal incontinence should aim to correct the underlying cause of incontinence whenever possible. Faecal impaction and overflow incontinence should be treated with regular phosphate or hypertonic enemas. In some cases manual evacuation of the rectum may be required. Adequate hydration and a high fibre diet should be encouraged in order to prevent recurrence.

Patients with faecal incontinence due to neurogenic causes may benefit from treatment with Loperamide which increases anal pressures. Regular toileting at a specified time every day may also help to re-establish continence. This intervention is most effective when the bowel training is tailored to mimic the patient's previous bowel habit. When medical management fails, different surgical procedures may be used for the treatment of faecal incontinence. These include external anal sphincter repair, mechanical tightening of the anus, e.g. with a silastic ring, implantation of an artificial anal sphincter and even colostomy. Surgical treatment should be considered only in the chronic stage of stroke because spontaneous recovery is possible in the first 6 months after the disease onset. Unfortunately most stroke patients are unlikely to be fit for such surgical procedures. In these cases the use of continence pads and other incontinence aids becomes the only realistic option.

COGNITIVE IMPAIRMENT IN STROKE

Cognitive impairment is a common consequence of stroke. In fact, cerebro-vascular disease is the third commonest cause of dementia after Alzheimer's disease and Lewy body dementia. It affects approximately 5% of older people. In addition, evidence of cognitive impairment would be expected in a quarter of patients aged 60 years or more when examined 3 months after they had a stroke. There is a strong association between vascular dementia (VD) and Alzheimer's disease (AD) and the two conditions often co-exist in the same patient. A higher incidence of AD has been reported in stroke patients compared to control populations matched for age and gender. On the other hand, post mortem studies have shown that the histopathological features of VD were frequently present in patients with AD. The significance of this association is not fully understood, but it has been suggested that stroke might accelerate the course of AD. In other words, subjects who are destined to have AD in later life develop symptoms of dementia at an earlier age if they also have cerebrovascular disease.

VD often follows thalamic and basal ganglia stroke and it is particularly common after repeated lacunar infarcts. Old age, a previous stroke, poorly controlled hypertension, diabetes mellitus, pre-existing cognitive impairment, radiological evidence of cerebral small vessel disease with or without multiple lacunar infarcts and current cigarette smoking are associated with a high risk of vascular dementia in stroke patients.

Diagnosis
The severity of post-stroke cognitive impairment ranges from mild disturbances of memory to overt dementia. Impairment of memory is usually the earliest and most frequently reported symptom. As the disease progresses patients develop symptoms that suggest further intellectual deterioration and changes in behaviour and personality. These features are common to all dementias, irrespective of the underlying cause. However, the mode of onset, the clinical course and the presence of focal neurological signs and their distribution help to distinguish VD from other types of dementia.

In contrast to Alzheimer's disease (which starts insidiously and progresses slowly), the onset of VD is acute and its course is stepwise. The patient usually presents with a focal neurological deficit and symptoms of mental confusion and cognitive impairment. A variable degree of recovery follows and the patient's cognitive state improves slightly or remains stable until the next vascular event. VD is usually characterised by less severe memory impairment and more pronounced difficulties with mental concentration than AD. Typically, the patient has a reduced verbal fluency, reduced reaction time, apathy and perseveration. Interestingly, social awareness is often more preserved in VD than in AD of the same severity.

The physical examination may confirm the presence of hemiparesis or other focal neurological signs that are consistent with brain damage in a vascular territory. Visuo-spatial deficits are common. In addition, evidence of longstanding hypertension or other risk factors for stroke is often present. The diagnosis may be confirmed with CT or MRI head scans. Typically, these investigations demonstrate the presence of multiple lacunar infarcts in the basal ganglia, internal capsule and centrum semiovale and widespread white matter changes.

The Hachinski Ischaemic Scale (HIS) is also helpful in differentiating between VD and AD. The scale consists of the following 13 items: abrupt onset, fluctuating course, history of strokes, focal neurological signs, focal neurological symptoms, stepwise deterioration, relative preservation of personality, nocturnal confusion, depression, somatic complaints, emotional lability, history of hypertension and evidence of atherosclerosis. Each of the first five items receives a score of 2 points and each of the remaining items receives a score of 1 point. HIS is reasonably sensitive. A total score of 7 or more distinguishes VD from AD in about 80% of cases.

Vascular dementia may also be confused with depressive illness. In fact, depressive symptoms are common in the early stages of VD when insight is still retained. However, a carefully taken history and physical examination usually reveal that the underlying problem in patients with primary depression is that of psychomotor retardation, rather than true cognitive impairment. Confirmation of the diagnosis of dementia can be made with psychometric tests, such as the Weschler Adult Intelligence Scale (WAIS).

Treatment
Treatment of the stroke risk factors and the use of anti-thrombotic therapy is the mainstay of management of VD. The calcium channel blocker, nimodipine, is sometimes used but there is no

good evidence of its effectiveness. Similarly, vasodilators, such as pentoxifylline and codergocrine (Hydergine), are probably of little clinical benefit.

Three acetylcholinesterase inhibitors (donepezil, rivastigmine and galantamine) have been shown to improve the symptoms of dementia or to reduce the rate of cognitive decline in patients with mild or moderately severe AD. However, their role in the management of VD is at present not fully clear.

Cognitive rehabilitation may help patients in the early stages of dementia, but is usually ineffective in advanced disease. The importance of the provision of practical and emotional support to the patients and their families and carers cannot be overemphasised. With adequate social support, including the provision of respite care, most patients with mild or moderately severe VD are capable of living in the community. However, institutional care is often necessary in the later stages of the disease.

The prognosis of severe VD is poor. It is associated with a higher risk of stroke recurrence, invariably results in functional dependency and also increases morbidity and mortality.

RECOMMENDED FURTHER READING

Language and speech disorders

Geschwind N, Quadfasel FA, Segarra JM. Isolation of the speech area. *Neuropsychologia* 1968; **6**: 327-240

Crosson B. Subcortical functions in language and memory. New York: Guilford Press, 1992

Kreisler A, Godefroy O, Delmaire C, Debachy B, Leclercq M, Pruvo J-P, Leys D. The anatomy of aphasia revisited. *Neurology* 2000; **54**: 1117-1123

Alexander PA, Naeser MA, Palumbo CL. Correlation of subcortical CT lesion sites and aphasia profiles. *Brain* 1987; **110**: 961-991

Albert ML, Bachman DL, Morgan A, Helm-Estabrooks N. Pharmacotherapy for aphasia. *Neurology* 1988; **38**: 877-879

Pulvermuller F, Neininger B, Elbert T, et al. Constraint-induced therapy of chronic aphasia after stroke. *Stroke* 2001; **32**: 1621-1626

Apraxia

Rothi LJ, Heilman (eds). Apraxia – The neuropsychology of action. Hove, East Sussex, UK: Psychology Press, 1997

Geschwind N. The apraxias: neural mechanisms of disorders of learned movement. *American Scientist* 1975; **63**: 188-195

Haaland KY, Harrington DL, Knight RT. Neural representations of skilled movement. *Brain* 2000; **123**: 2306-2313

Butler JA. How comparable are tests of apraxia. *Clinical Rehabilitation* 2002; **16**: 389-398

Van Heugten CM, Dekker J, Deelman BG, et al. A diagnostic test for apraxia in stroke patients: internal consistency and diagnostic value. *The Clinical Neuropsychologist* 1999; **13**: 182-192

Van Heugten CM, Dekker J, Deelman BG, et al. Outcome of strategy training in stroke patients with apraxia: a phase II study. *Clinical Rehabilitation* 1998; **12**: 294-303

Unilateral hemispatial neglect

Ellis S, Small M. Localization of lesion in denial of hemiplegia after stroke. *Stroke* 1997; **28**: 67-71

Stone SP, Halligan PW, Wilson B, Greenwood RJ. Performance of age matched controls on a battery of visuospatial neglect tests. *Journal of Neurology, Neurosurgery & Psychiatry* 1991; **55**: 341-344

Geminiani G, Bottini G, Sterzi R. Dopaminergic stimulation in unilateral neglect. *Journal of Neurology, Neurosurgery & Psychiatry* 1998; **65**: 344-347

Robertson IH, Halligan PW. *Spatial neglect: a clinical handbook for diagnosis and treatment.* Hove: Psychology Press, 1999

Robertson IH & Marshall JC (eds). *Unilateral neglect: clinical and experimental studies.* Hove, East Sussex, UK: Lawrence Erlbaum Associates Ltd, 1993

Kinsbourne M. Mechanisms of unilteral neglect. In: M. Jeannerod (Ed), *Neurophysiological and neuropsychological aspects of unilteral neglect.* Amsterdam: North-Holland, 1987, pp 69-86

Bowen A, Lincoln NB, Dewey M. Cognitive rehabilitation for spatial neglect following stroke. *Cochrane Database of Systematic Reviews* 2002; (2): CD 003586

IMPAIRMENTS OF VISUAL FUNCTION
Markowitz SN. Principles of modern low vision rehabilitation. *Canadian Journal of Ophthalmology* 2006; **41**: 289-312

Kerkoff G. Restorative and compensatory therapy approaches in cerebral blindness – a review. *Restorative Neurology & Neuroscience* 1999; **15**: 255-271

Nelles G, Esser J, Eckstein A, Tiede A, Gerhard H, Diener HC. Compensatory visual field training for patients with hemianopia after stroke. *Neuroscience Letters* 2001; **306**: 189-192

Motor weakness
Demeurisse G, Demol O, Robaye E. Motor evaluation in motor hemiplegia. *European Neurology* 1980; **19:** 382-389

Bobath B. *Adult hemiplegia: evaluation and treatment.* Third edition. Oxford: Butterworth-Heinmann Ltd, 1990

Duncan P. Synthesis of intervention trials to improve motor recovery following stroke. *Topics in Stroke Rehabilitation* 1997; **3:** 1-20

Langhammer B, Stanghelle JK. Bobath or motor relearning programme? A comparison of two different approaches of physiotherapy in stroke rehabilitation: a randomised controlled study. *Clinical Rehabilitation* 2000; **14**: 361-369

Nudo RJ, Wise BM, SiFuentes F, Milliken GW. Neural substrates for the effects of rehabilatative training on motor recovery after ischaemic infarct. *Science* 1996; **272**: 1791-1794

Bladder and bowel dysfunction
Sandvik H, Hunskaar S, Seim A, Hermstad R, Vanvik A, Bratt H. Validation of a severity index in female urinary incontinence and its implementation in an epidemiological survey. *Journal of Epidemiology & Community Health* 1993; **47**: 497-499

Gelber DA, Good DC, Laven LJ, Verhulst SJ. Causes of urinary incontinence after acute hemishperic stroke. *Stroke* 1993; **24:** 378-382

Nakayama H, Jorgensen HS, Pedersen PM, Raaschou HO, Olsen TS. Prevalence and risk factors of incontinence after stroke. *Stroke* 1997; **28**: 58-62

Sakakibara R, Hattori T, Yasuda K, Yamanishi T. Micturitional disturbance after acute hemispheric stroke: analysis of the lesion site by CT and MRI. *Journal of the Neurological Sciences* 1996; **137**: 47-56

Cooper ZR, Rose S. Fecal incontinence: a clinical approach. *The Mount Sinai Journal of Medicine* 2000; **67**: 96-105

Cognitive impairment in stroke
Kase CS, Wolf PA, Kelly-Hayes M, et al. Intellectual decline after stroke: the Framingham study. *Stroke* 1998; **29**: 805-812

Victoroff J, Mack WJ, Lyness SC, Chui HC. Multicenter clinico-pathological correlation in dementia. *American Journal of Psychiatry* 1995; **152**: 1476-1484

American Psychiatric Association: Practice guideline for the treatment of patients with Alzheimer's disease and other dementias of late life. *American Journal of Psychiatry* 1997; **154**: 1-39

CHAPTER FOUR

PREVENTION AND TREATMENT OF THE COMMON COMPLICATIONS OF STROKE

Difficulties with swallowing, impairment of motor and sensory function and disorders of cognition and perception are common after stroke. The complications arising from these impairments include pulmonary aspiration due to severe dysphagia, fixed contractures secondary to muscle hypertonia, shoulder dislocation, deep vein thrombosis and pulmonary thrombo-embolism and depression. Some of these complications are life threatening and all of them can slow the patient's functional recovery. The mortality and morbidity associated with stroke is reduced when these complications are recognised early and treated effectively.

DYSPHAGIA

Normal swallowing depends on the anatomical and functional integrity of numerous neural structures and extensive pathways in the central and peripheral nervous system. Ischaemic lesions or haemorrhage in the cerebral cortex, basal ganglia, brain stem or cerebellum may interrupt these pathways. This explains the high incidence of dysphagia in patients with stroke.

One in three patients with acute stroke would be expected to have significant difficulties with swallowing. Dysphagia in these patients is usually associated with hemiplegia due to lesions of the brain stem or the involvement of one or both hemispheres. However, on rare occasions, dysphagia may be the sole manifestation of a cerebrovascular event. Dysphagia in the absence of other neurological symptoms and signs has been reported in patients with lacunar infarcts in the periventricular white matter and following discrete vascular brain stem lesions. Post-stroke dysphagia predominantly affects the oro-pharyngeal phase of swallowing and is caused by weakness of the oral musculature and sluggish tongue movements, failure to form a cohesive food bolus, reduced sensitivity of the pharyngeal receptors and bucco-lingual apraxia.

Several drugs may also precipitate or aggravate swallowing difficulties in some stroke patients. The mechanisms implicated in this are diverse and include depression of the level of consciousness (sedatives and hypnotics), interference with the oro-pharyngeal phase of swallowing (e.g. neuroleptic agents) and poor preparation of the food bolus due to xerostomia caused by anticholinergic drugs.

Dysphagia resulting from stroke is usually transient. Recovery of the swallowing ability occurs in almost 90% of cases within 2 to 4 weeks. However, the symptoms persist in about 8% of patients for six months or more. The occurrence of dysphagia in acute stroke does not appear to depend on the size or the site of the brain lesion. Interestingly, when dysphagia persists for a month or more after the stroke onset it is usually associated with right parietal lobe involvement.

Despite its relatively good prognosis, post-stroke dysphagia may result in serious complications, including pulmonary aspiration, dehydration and malnutrition. These complications are usually preventable if the dysphagia is recognised early and managed appropriately.

The clinical manifestations of dysphagia
Acutely ill stroke patients with mild or moderately severe dysphagia may not be aware of their swallowing difficulties. In the post acute stage some of these patients would avoid certain foods which they find difficult to chew or swallow. Weight loss may be an early feature in some cases. Excessive flow and drooling of saliva (sialorrhoea) occurs in dysphagic patients when they are sitting up and aspiration of saliva is common in the recumbent position, especially during sleep. Occasionally interrupted sleep may be the only indication of swallowing difficulties. Pain on swallowing (odynophagia) is not a symptom of neurogenic dysphagia and suggests a diagnosis of oesophagitis, usually secondary to candida infections. Nasal regurgitation of fluids occurs when palatal weakness is present.

Assessment
An interdisciplinary team approach is essential for the optimal assessment and treatment of patients with neurogenic dysphagia. The core team should consist of a healthcare professional trained in dysphagia management (usually a speech and language therapist or a nurse), a dietician and a physician.

Assessment of swallowing function should start with a careful examination of the oral cavity. Some causes of dysphagia, such as mouth ulcers, oral thrush, xerostomia and deviation of the soft palate are readily visible on inspection of the patient's mouth. Neurological examination may confirm the presence of bulbar or pseudobulbar palsy or weakness of the oro-buccal muscles on the hemiplegic side.

The presence of dysphagia and its severity can then be assessed at the bedside by observing the patient during "trial swallows". Swallowing behaviour can be observed while the subject is taking food and fluids of different consistencies under 'normal' everyday conditions. Coughing, splattering or choking whilst eating are obvious signs of dysphagia. Change in the pattern of breathing or change in voice quality may also occur. Some patients attempt to compensate for their swallowing difficulties by taking small, frequent drinks during the meal in order to 'wash down' the food bolus. Inspection of the oral cavity usually reveals pooling of secretions or food residue in the mouth.

Initial screening for dysphagia may be attempted with the "swallow test" described by Crockford and Smithard. This procedure has good sensitivity and specificity and can be completed in a few minutes. The test is carried out with the patient sitting upright. The patient, who must be fully alert, is asked to drink three spoonfuls of water. The examiner places a finger above and below the larynx to feel for laryngeal movements with each swallow. Absent swallow movements, a cough or a "wet" voice suggest the presence of dysphagia. If the patient's swallow appears good the clinician then proceeds to the next stage of the test. The patient is asked to drink a third of a glass of water. Finally, trial feeding could be started under the supervision of an experienced clinician if there are no signs of severe dysphagia.

Measurement of the swallowing speed is another simple bedside test for the evaluation of neurogenic dysphagia. The test, which has been shown to be specific and sensitive, consists of measuring the speed with which the patient drinks 150ml of cold tap water while sitting up. A swallowing speed of less than 10ml/s suggests the presence of dysphagia. These tests have obvious advantages over other methods of assessment such as videofluoroscopy and nasendescopy, especially when regular and frequent monitoring of the patient's condition is necessary.

Videofluoroscopy is considered the gold standard for the evaluation of dysphagia. It permits the observation of the oral preparatory phase, the reflex initiation of swallowing and the pharyngeal transit of the food bolus. However, it is not suitable for repeated assessments because of the undesirability of frequent exposure to radiation and the cost of the procedure. In addition, it does not assess the swallow function in 'normal' everyday conditions. An alternative method is fiberoptic nasendoscopy. This procedure consists of introducing an endoscope through the nose into the nasopharynx and placing the tip of the endoscope just above the soft palate. The patient is then given food and drink coloured with a dye and pre- and post-swallowing pharyngeal pooling is observed. Nasal endoscopy is a reliable method for the assessment of swallowing function and of the risk of pulmonary aspiration, but special expertise is necessary to carry out the procedure and to interpret its results.

Another useful method for the bedside diagnosis of dysphagia and pulmonary aspiration is pulse oximetry. The use of this method is based on the premise that aspiration of food or fluid into the airways causes reflex bronchoconstriction that leads to ventilation-perfusion mismatch. The resulting oxygen desaturation of arterial blood can be readily measured with pulse oximetry. Pulse oximetry has been shown to predict aspiration, or the lack of it, in more than 80% of dysphagic stroke patients. This method is non-invasive, quick to do and repeatable but its results must be interpreted with caution in smokers (high carboxyhaemoglobin concentrations may give false negative results) and in those with chronic lung disease. The information derived from pulse oximetry is reliable only if meticulous attention is given to the test procedure. Measurement errors are minimised when the test is carried out in a warm, dimly lighted room.

Other investigations of swallowing disorders, such as oesophageal manometry (which enables the measurements of the intraoesophagel pressure gradient and is useful in the evaluation of dysfunction of the circopharyngeus muscle and abnormalities of oesophageal motility), are rarely needed in the assessment of post-stroke dysphagia.

Differential diagnosis
A careful medical history and physical examination (supplemented by special investigations in some cases) are necessary to establish the cause of the swallowing difficulty and to exclude coincidental dysphagia due to obstructive lesions and other non-neurological causes. Obstructive lesions of the oesophagus usually cause slowly progressive dysphagia. Typically, the patient reports difficulties with swallowing solid food in the early stages. This may progress over weeks or months to dysphagia to semi-solid food. In the final phase even fluids become difficult to swallow. In contrast to dysphagia due to oesophageal strictures or tumours, patients

with neurogenic dysphagia usually find fluids more difficult to swallow than solids. This is probably because a solid (and more cohesive) food bolus is more likely to result in adequate pharyngeal stimulation and thus triggers a swallow reflex.

Dysphagia resulting from a discrete brain stem vascular lesion or from confluent periventricular infarction usually affects predominantly the volitional initiation of swallowing and spares reflexive deglutition. In these circumstances the patient's symptoms may be ascribed to globus hystericus. However, in the latter condition a 'lump in the throat' is a characteristic complaint and the symptoms are usually associated with severe emotional distress. Patients with globus hystericus have a normal bolus transit time and seldom complain of difficulties with eating or drinking.

The complications of dysphagia
A serious complication of dysphagia is pulmonary aspiration. Severe swallowing difficulties, even for relatively short periods, may also lead to dehydration, reduced calorie intake and malnutrition.

Pulmonary aspiration is defined as the penetration of food or fluid into the airways below the true vocal cords. It may cause severe morbidity and sometimes mortality. About a third of patients with dysphagia aspirate food or fluid into their airways and in 40% of them aspiration is silent, i.e. it does not trigger coughing or cause symptoms or signs of distress. Paradoxically, aspirating patients frequently do not complain of swallowing difficulties and there are no reliable clinical signs of this complication. Interestingly, a weak cough, which is generally associated with the ability to protect the airways, is more likely to be present in aspirating rather than non-aspirating dysphagic patients. Similarly, a diminished or absent gag reflex does not differentiate aspirating from non-aspirating patients. The detection of silent aspiration, therefore, depends largely on a high index of clinical suspicion and may be confirmed by non-invasive bedside investigations, such as pulse oximetry.

Management of post-stroke dysphagia
The aim of management is to prevent pulmonary aspiration, to maintain adequate food and fluid intake and to correct nutritional deficiencies when present. Oral feeding has important social and psychological significance to patients and their families and should be continued whenever possible. In some patients oral

intake is often not adequate even in the absence of significant swallowing difficulties. This may be due to excessive fatigue or cognitive impairment. In these patients oral food intake may be supplemented with gastrostomy tube feeding. It is preferable that such supplements are given at night. Withholding morning gastrostomy feeds usually stimulates the patient's appetite.

In some patients dysphagia may result from poor preparation of the food bolus because of ill-fitting dentures or due to disease of the oral cavity, such as mouth ulcers or candida infections. These causes should be routinely looked for and treated when present. Care should be taken to avoid feeding when the patient is tired or distracted (e.g. while watching television). Talking whilst eating also increases the risk of aspiration and patients (and their carers) should be made aware of this. It is sometimes useful to plan the timing of meals so that they coincide with periods when the patient's functional abilities are maximal, for example after a period of rest. In dysphagic patients who have a tracheostomy occlusion of the stoma with a speaking valve during swallowing reduces the risk of pulmonary aspiration presumably by normalising the pressure in the upper airways. The effects of posture on swallowing are well recognised. Adoption of different postures may be used to facilitate swallowing. For example, 'chin tuck' decreases the pharyngeal transit time of the food bolus, whereas 'chin up' has the opposite effect. Head tilt to one side to maximise the effect of gravity on the unaffected side of pharynx is also a useful strategy in some cases.

It has been shown that patients with weak tongue movements and those with poor pharyngeal clearance of the food bolus benefit from the use of gravity and posture to facilitate safe swallowing. Lying down on one side (at 45 degrees from flat) may be associated with less risk of aspiration than feeding in the upright position.

Drooling of saliva is common in severely dysphagic patients. Frequent suction of copious saliva may be necessary in these cases. Injection of botulinum toxin type A into the salivary glands is usually effective. It has been reported that this treatment is most effective when 100 units of Dysport (or an equivalent dose of Botox) is injected into the submandibular gland and another 50 units into the parotid glands. However, we found that an injection of 150 units of Dysport into the parotid gland on each side was sufficient to control the sialorrhoea in most patients. This is preferable to the above protocol, as the injection of the submandibular gland needs to be done under ultrasound control. The sublingual salivary glands are normally not injected in order to avoid severe xerostomia. Treatment of sialorrhoea with anticholinergic drugs, such as hyoscine patches, should be avoided because of their potential systemic adverse effects, including the central anticholinergic syndrome (hallucinations, mental confusion, drowsiness or hyperactivity and ataxia).

Review of the patient's medication

Sedatives, hypnotic drugs and tranquillisers often reduce the patient's level of arousal and render swallowing unsafe. They should not be used whenever possible. Anticholinergic drugs, e.g. Hyoscine patches, are sometimes prescribed for dysphagic patients with excessive drooling of saliva. Drooling of saliva in these patients is due to difficulties with swallowing and not because of its excessive production. Consequently, these drugs should be avoided as they can aggravate dysphagia by increasing the viscosity of oral secretions. Similarly, antihistamines and tricyclic antidepressants also increase the viscosity of oral secretions. Viscid oral secretions interfere with bolus preparation and predispose to the formation of a mucous plug. Dehydration, e.g. due to the use of diuretics, may also have a similar effect. The antiemetics prochlorperazine and metoclopramide may occasionally cause orofacial dyskinesia and this could result in dysphagia or aggravate pre-existing swallowing difficulties.

Dietary modification

Maintenance of hydration and nutrition can be achieved safely in most patients with neurogenic dysphagia with dietary modification. Simple, but effective, measures include avoidance of dry and sticky food and eating food with uniform consistency. The use of starch-based fluid thickeners, e.g. 'Thick and Easy' and Vitaquick, is also an important management strategy. Tube feeding is usually required in only a minority of patients.

Patients with neurogenic dysphagia usually experience more difficulties with fluids than with solid food. This is probably due to the difficulty in controlling a thin bolus and/or a delay or absence of triggering the swallow reflex. The rationale for the use of fluid thickeners is that by increasing the viscosity of ingested fluids the resistance to flow of the bolus is increased. In addition, the duration of cricopharyngeal opening and the oro-pharyngeal transit time are increased. Thickening of fluids improves swallowing. However, the optimal viscosity of fluids that ensures safe swallowing in patients with neurogenic dysphagia has not been established. In practice the required fluid thickness is judged subjectively and recorded using descriptive terms, such as syrup or yoghurt consistency. This has the disadvantage that fluids with low viscosity may be served which can result in pulmonary aspiration. On the other hand, fluids that are too thick usually become unpalatable and are often rejected by patients leading to dehydration.

Tube feeding
The direct delivery of nutrients into the stomach (or rarely into the jejunum) via a feeding tube is frequently used as the sole method of nutritional support of severely dysphagic patients who are at risk of pulmonary aspiration if fed orally. It is suggested that tube feeding should be considered if the subject aspirates as little as 10% or more of the food bolus or shows evidence of slow transit of the food bolus i.e. more than 10 seconds, on videofluoroscopy. However, in practice the decision to recommend tube feeding is usually made without prior investigations with videofluoroscopy. Tube feeding may also be considered in the absence of pulmonary aspiration. For example, in cases when easy fatigability makes swallowing unsafe, tube feeding can be used to supplement the daily oral intake. The patient will then be able to take his favourite foods orally and the rest of the calorie requirements is given through the tube.

The use of a gastrostomy tube is preferred to naso-oesophageal intubation, especially when dysphagia is expected to be present for more than a few days. Nasogastric tube (NGT) feeding is usually poorly tolerated and may make the patient irritable or even agitated. Removal of the tube by patients is common and the volume of feeds delivered in this way is usually not adequate. Frequently only half the required daily nutritional intake can be delivered using an NGT. When NGT feeding is prescribed the use of fine bore tubes, e.g. Ryle's tube, is preferred to large bore ones. However, fine bore tubes are more likely to dislodge, kink or block. They also deliver feeds at a relatively slow rate.

Occasionally patients with stroke develop gastrointestinal ileus and in these patients enteral nutrition could be established with the intrajejunal administration of low residue feeds. Duodenal intubation may be facilitated by an intravenous injection of 20mg of metoclopramide a few minutes before the procedure. (Metoclopramide increases stomach peristalsis and relaxes the pyloric sphincter).

Prolonged NGT feeding is not desirable. It often results in numerous complications including nasopharyngitis, oesophagitis, oesophageal strictures, epistaxis, pneumothorax and nasopharyngeal oedema with associated otitis media. In addition, NGT feeding does not fully protect against aspiration and the association between NGT feeding and this complication is well documented. Nearly half dysphagic patients aspirate in the first two weeks after NGT feeding is commenced. Elevation of the head of the bed during and for 1-2 hours after bolus NGT gastric and intrajejunal feeding reduces the risk of aspiration in these patients.

Feeding via a gastrostomy tube should be considered when dysphagia is likely to persist for long periods. There are no clinical signs or laboratory tests at present that can reliably predict the speed or extent of recovery from dysphagia after stroke. Most clinicians would consider gastrostomy tube feeding in stroke patients if there are no signs of recovery of safe swallowing after the first 7-10 days. In some patients with partial recovery of swallowing the option of percutaneous endoscopic gastrostomy (PEG) tube feeding should be offered early after the onset of dysphagia to supplement the oral intake and help maintain adequate nutrition. Insertion of the feeding tube through a PEG, rather than a surgical gastrostomy, is a relatively simple, safe and cost effective technique. PEG tube feeding is effective and is usually acceptable to patients and their carers. Transient, self-limiting abdominal pain and diarrhoea may occur in the early post-operative period. Long-term complications include tube obstruction and wound infection.

In some patients who are fed via a PEG tube pulmonary aspiration may occur and routine intrajejunal feeding has been suggested for these cases. However, technically it is easier to insert a gastric tube than to introduce an intrajejunal feeding tube. An additional advantage of bolus gastric tube feeding is that it is more physiological, particularly with respect to insulin secretion. Furthermore, because the feeds can be given intermittently it allows greater patient freedom (intrajejunal feeding should be given continuously rather than intermittently). The direct intrajejunal delivery of nutrients should probably be reserved for patients with gastro-oesophageal reflux, hiatus hernia or recurrent aspiration on gastrostomy feeding.

Enteral feeding can be started a few hours after the insertion of the PEG tube. The volume of feed is usually restricted in the first 24 hours to one litre and is given at a rate of 50ml/hr. The volume of feed and the rate of its administration are then gradually increased over the following 3-4 days until the patient's daily nutritional requirements are met. Some clinicians prescribe 'starter feeding regimens' in the first postoperative week. These are feeds diluted with sterile water. The concentration and osmolality are gradually increased over several days to full strength feeds. Starter regimes with clear water or diluted enteral solutions are thought to improve tolerance to feeds and reduce diarrhoea, but this has not been unequivocally confirmed. It is also worth remembering that dilution of feeds (as used in starter regimes) significantly reduces the patient's nutritional intake. Diarrhoea in patients on enteral feeding is often due to treatment with antibiotics for coincidental infections, bacterial contamination of the feed and bolus feeding (the use of entral feeding pumps to control the rate of feeding may prevent diarrhoea, nausea and vomiting).

The type of feed should be chosen to meet the patient's nutritional needs. Commercially available standard feeds (1 Kcal/ml) provide balanced nutrition and are suitable for most patients. High energy feeds (1.5 Kcal/ml) are useful in cases where the nutritional requirements are high or when it is desirable to reduce the feeding time, e.g. so that the patient can engage in therapy. High fibre feeds are indicated if constipation is a problem. Liquidised ordinary food can be used instead of the commercially available feeds, but this is not advisable because of the risk of bacterial contamination.

Bolus feeding (e.g. 250 ml every 4 hours) is preferable to continuous or cyclic feeding because it is more physiological and also allows the patient more freedom to mobilise or engage in other activities. It is the method of choice in patients who are recovering from dysphagia and are being weaned from tube feeding because long periods without feeding result in hunger and stimulate appetite. However, a disadvantage of bolus feeding is that it is sometimes poorly tolerated, especially early after the insertion of a PEG feeding tube. It may cause abdominal distension and regurgitation. In these cases cyclic feeding over 8-10 hours during the night is a good alternative. Continuous feeding is suitable for patients with intrajejunal tubes.

Swallowing therapy
A range of remedial therapies and training in the use of compensatory strategies may be helpful in the treatment of neurogenic dysphagia. These include exercises to strengthen the orofacial musculature, manoeuvres to improve poor laryngeal elevation and laryngeal closure during swallowing and techniques to stimulate the swallow reflex. The latter methods are usually used before starting direct swallowing practice.

Exercises to enhance the function of the orofacial muscles are used to improve lip seal, chewing and tongue movements. A simple technique known as 'the supraglottic swallow' may improve the elevation and closure of the larynx during swallowing. During this manoeuvre the subject holds his breath and swallow and then releases the air by coughing. Patients with delayed or absent swallow reflex may benefit from thermal stimulation of the oropharyngeal receptors. The procedure has been claimed to improve triggering of the swallowing action and to reduce the bolus transit time. It involves the repeated application to the anterior faucial arch of a small laryngeal mirror dipped in ice. Sensitisation may be repeated between swallows. Direct swallowing therapy can be started with small amounts of food (of the right consistency) under the supervision of an experienced clinician when the risk of pulmonary aspiration is deemed to be low.

The surgical treatment of neurogenic dysphagia

Cricopharyngeal myotomy has been shown to be an effective method of treatment of dysphagia in a number of neurological disorders including stroke, muscular dystrophy and a significant proportion of patients with motor neurone disease. However, careful selection of patients for this procedure is essential and two conditions must be satisfied. First, failure of relaxation of the pharyngeal sphincter must be demonstrated on videofluoroscopy. Secondly, the oral phase of swallowing i.e. lip seal, voluntary initiation of swallowing and the propulsive action of the tongue must also be preserved. Poor tongue movements (demonstrated on videofluoroscopy by the inability to propel or retrieve the food bolus) is a contraindication to cricopharyngeal myotomy. Patients with absent pharyngeal peristalsis or delayed triggering of the swallow reflex by 10 seconds or more are also unlikely to benefit from this treatment. Surgery for cricopharyngeal dysfunction following stroke should be considered only if the symptoms persist after the first three months of the disease onset.

Relaxation of the cricopharyngeus can also be achieved with 'chemical cricopharyngeal myotomy'; using botulinum toxin injections. The location of the cricopharyngeal muscle is determined with direct oesophagoscopy and electromyography (using a hooked wire electrode) and the toxin is injected transcutaneously into the dorsomedial part and into the ventrolateral part of the muscle on both sides. A total dose of botulinum toxin type A (Dysport) of 80-120 units (or an equivalent dose of Botox) is usually sufficient and the mean beneficial effect of treatment is five months. The procedure usually requires a light general anaesthetic.

DISTURBANCES OF MOOD AND EMOTIONS

Major and minor mood disorders are common after stroke. Depression has been reported in 22-47% of stroke patients in large cohort studies. However, it is possible that some of these studies may have over-reported the incidence of this complication as a result of using questionnaires to diagnose depression, rather than formal psychiatric examination. Nonetheless, it is probably a reasonable estimate that at least a fifth of stroke patients develop symptoms of major depression. Anxiety often coexists with depression. Irritability, impulsivity, and emotional lability may also occur. Mania and symptoms similar to those of post-traumatic stress disorder have occasionally been reported in acute stroke in patients with no past history of mental illness.

The incidence of depression appears to correlate with the initial severity of stroke and the degree of the subsequent functional recovery, especially in the early period after stroke. Several studies have suggested that depression is more common and usually more severe after anterior cortical and subcortical left hemisphere stroke than in those with right hemisphere and posterior circulation stroke. However, other studies have failed to confirm the association between a specific lesion location and the occurrence of depression or other psychiatric morbidity.

The mechanisms of depression after stroke are not entirely clear. The grievance for the functional loss, altered family and social roles and perceived low self-worth as a result of disability may be important factors in the aetio-pathogenesis of post-stroke depression. It is also possible that depletion of monoamine neurotransmitters due to disruption of neuronal function is another significant factor. Anxiety after a cerebrovascular event is often attributed to fear of death or worries about having another stroke, fear of abandonment by a spouse, or feeling of helplessness. Sometimes it is a plea by the patient for attention.

The typical symptoms of depression, when present, are usually evident in the first few weeks after stroke. However, in some cases they may be delayed and are reported by patients several weeks or months after stroke due to either initial denial or poor insight. A clinical diagnosis of depression is made if the patient has a combination of easily recognisable symptoms (see table 4.1). However, some of these symptoms, such as fatigue and poor mental concentration, can be due to the stroke itself, rather than an indication of underlying depression. In some patients the recognition of depression is also confounded by difficulties with the interpretation of the patient's stroke symptoms. For example, damage to the right hemisphere often leads to poor emotional gesturing which can be misinterpreted as lack of affect. Similarly, the monotonous dysporosodic speech and the reduced verbal fluency that often occur in stroke patients can also be confused for depression. In these and similar cases a number of other clinical features may also suggest the presence of depression. These features are:

- Poor, delayed or erratic functional recovery and the persistence of disability that is disproportionate to the severity of the neurological deficit.
- Unexplained functional deterioration after an initial good improvement.
- Refusal of therapy or "difficult" behaviour.
- Emotional lability, i.e. pathological laughing and crying, in the absence of pseudobulbar palsy.

Table 4.1- The American Psychiatric Association diagnostic criteria for depression*

1. Abnormal low mood** 2. Anhedonia, i.e. abnormal loss in pleasure** 3. Morbid thoughts of death or suicide 4. Inappropriate guilt and self-reproach 5. Excessive fatigue 6. Sleep disturbance 7. Behavioural disturbances, e.g. agitation or retardation 8. Poor mental concentration 9. Disturbances of appetite and body weight * Five or more of the above symptoms including either 1 or 2 are required for the diagnosis of major depression, <5 for minor depression and <3 (but present for r2 years) for dysthymia. ** low mood and anhedonia should be present almost every day for most of the day for at least 2 weeks.

The impact of severe or moderately severe depression on recovery after stroke is well documented. Depressed patients respond less favourably to therapeutic interventions than those who are not depressed, presumably because the hopelessness associated with depression has a de-motivating effect. On the other hand, remission from depression has been shown to correlate with more functional independence with activities of daily living. The early recognition and adequate treatment of poststroke depression is therefore an important part of the overall patient care.

Although psychotherapy is usually effective in mild depression, drug treatment is almost always necessary in cases of severe or moderately severe depression. As a rule, the selective serotonin reuptake inhibitors are better tolerated than tricyclic antidepressants, but the latter tend to be more effective. The beneficial effect of antidepressant drugs is usually observed 2-3 weeks after the start of therapy. However, if the patient's symptoms persist after 4-6 weeks of treatment with the appropriate drug dose, change of the antidepressant medication should be considered. It is recommended that the antidepressant treatment is continued for at least 6 months after the complete recovery from depression. Earlier withdrawal of treatment may precipitate a relapse of symptoms. The withdrawal of antidepressant drugs should be gradual over several weeks. Abrupt cessation of treatment should be avoided, except when serious adverse effects develop.

SHOULDER PAIN

Over half the patients with hemiplegic stroke would be expected to have shoulder pain. Although the mechanisms of post-stroke shoulder pain are poorly understood, several factors have been implicated in its causation. In acute and subacute hemiplegia pain is usually associated with antero-inferior shoulder dislocation or subluxation and is more common in patients with low muscle tone in the paralysed arm than in those with muscle spasticity. In some patients a rotator cuff tear, tendinitis or, less often, reflex sympathetic dystrophy may also cause shoulder pain. Pain due to adhesive capsulitis (frozen shoulder syndrome) usually occurs in the chronic phase of stroke. Post-stroke shoulder pain often interferes with the patient's rehabilitation, impedes motor function and causes difficulties with the execution of activities of daily living. It may also increase the burden of nursing care and prolong the patient's stay in hospital.

Shoulder dislocation and rotator cuff tears
Age-related degenerative changes in the shoulder joint, such as atrophy and calcification of the rotator cuff, osteophyte formation in the acromioclavicular joint and thickening of the joint capsule, are common after the sixth decade of life. These changes are thought to play an important role in the development of post-stroke shoulder pain. A number of factors also predispose to shoulder dislocation in hemiplegics. These include severe motor weakness, flaccid muscle tone or spasticity, careless lifting of the hemiplegic patient and poor handling and positioning of the paralysed upper limb. Patients with unilateral hemispatial neglect, anosognosia for hemiplegia or cognitive impairment are particularly vulnerable to this complication.

Patients with shoulder dislocation complain of acute pain at rest and during upper limb movements. The diagnosis is usually obvious as the displacement of the humeral head is easily felt on palpation of the subacromial space and is confirmed with antero-posterior and oblique plain X-rays taken with the patient standing. Pain in the hemiplegic shoulder may also result from rotator cuff tears and tendonitis. However, in contrast to shoulder dislocation, the passive external rotation of the shoulder in patients with a rotator cuff tear or tendinitis does not induce pain.

Prevention of shoulder dislocation and rotator cuff tears through the correct positioning of the flaccid, weak upper limb is an essential part of the nursing care for stroke patients. Hospital staff and carers should be instructed on the correct methods of lifting the patient. The use of overhead exercise pulleys should be avoided, as it may precipitate or aggravate the age-related damage of the shoulder soft tissues. During sitting the paretic arm should be supported with a shoulder sling when shoulder subluxation is present. Alternatively, an axillary foam roll and harness (Bobath sling), or an arm cuff with a figure-of-eight strap may be used. At all times it is important to maintain the arm slightly abducted with the shoulder protracted, i.e. thrust forward. In the absence of subluxation or dislocation it is usually sufficient to support the arm on a lap tray or an arm trough attached to the wheelchair during sitting. When lying in bed the patient's arm should be abducted and slightly externally rotated and the shoulder protracted. These measures, if followed meticulously, are usually adequate for the prevention of post-stroke shoulder pain.

Treatment of shoulder dislocation consists of pain relief, and the correct positioning and the protective support of the paralysed upper limb. When these measures are insufficient, high intensity transcutaneous electrical stimulation (TENS), i.e. TENS using a stimulus of sufficient strength to cause a muscle contraction, has been shown to give good pain relief and to improve the range of passive shoulder movements if given for 4-6 weeks.

Frozen shoulder syndrome
In the subacute and chronic phase of stroke many patients develop the frozen shoulder syndrome (FSS). The FSS is usually associated with spasticity and is characterised by pain and severe restriction in the range of active and passive movements of the shoulder, especially external rotation, in the absence of systemic symptoms of inflammation. Severe hypertonia of the pectoralis

126

major muscle and/ or the subscapularis is usually the main cause of the shoulder pain and the restriction of the range of movement at the shoulder joint. The contribution of the other muscles that assist in shoulder adduction and internal rotation, such as the infraspinatus, teres major and the coracobrachialis, seems to be less important.

Several strategies may be used for the treatment of the FSS. Physiotherapy to mobilise the shoulder, usually combined with the use of non-steroidal anti inflammatory drugs, ultrasound, laser or TENS, is considered the first line of treatment. In resistant cases peri-articular or intra-articular injections of lignocaine are often effective. A combination of lignocaine and a corticosteroid (e.g. triamcinolone acetonide, 40mg) is also frequently used and is particularly beneficial if secondary soft tissue inflammation is present. Pain relief may also be achieved with suprascapular nerve blocks. Occasionally, shoulder manipulation under general anaesthesia is carried out, but this procedure may cause shoulder dislocation, brachial plexus traction injury or rotator cuff tears. Severe hypertonia of the pectoralis major muscle and/ or the subscapularis should be treated.

Injections of botulinum toxin type A into the pectoralis major muscle and the subscapularis offer good symptomatic relief that usually lasts three months or more. The procedure is quite simple. For injection of the pectoralis major the limb should be flexed at 90 degrees and the shoulder abducted and externally rotated, a dose of 300 units of Dysport (or 100 units of Botox) is injected into the muscle belly, approximately 3 cm medial to the axillary crease.

Injection of the subscapularis muscle is made with the upper limb flexed 90° at the shoulder joint and the arm abducted and externally rotated in the same way as for the injection of the pectoralis major. The subscapularis is seen as the medial part of the posterior wall of the axilla. The needle should be placed in the middle of the muscle. A dose of 250 units of Dysport (or 80 units of Botox) is usually sufficient for the treatment of the spastic hemiplegic shoulder. An alternative injection technique of the subscapularis is to insert the needle through the medial scapular border at the level of the spine of the scapula so that the needle runs along the costal (anterior) aspect of the scapula. The procedure is carried out with the patient sitting up with the arm held tightly against the trunk.

Reflex sympathetic dystrophy
Reflex sympathetic dystrophy (RSD), also known as shoulder-hand syndrome, algodystrophy or complex regional pain syndrome type one, is a relatively rare complication of stroke. It tends to occur in the first 3 months of the cerebrovascular event. In contrast to simple hand oedema, it is chatacterised by severe pain in the shoulder and wrist, hyperaesthesia and swelling of the hand and forearm. Typically, the pain and swelling spare the elbow and the metacarpals are only slightly affected. In the early stages the forearm, wrist and hand are red, oedematous and sweaty. With the onset of the chronic phase the limb becomes cold and cyanosed. The skin atrophies and the hyperhydrosis subsides. Localised osteoparosis (Sudeck's atrophy) is often another feature at this stage. RSD is thought to be due to autonomic dysregulation and decreased vasomotor tone. It is usually triggered by trauma.

The mainstay of treatment of RSD is physiotherapy and pain relief. Oral steroids may be effective. It has also been reported that intramuscular injections of salmon calcitonin (100 IU daily for 4 weeks), in addition to physiotherapy, reduces pain and increases the joint range of motion. In severe, resistant cases chemical sympathectomy with alcohol or phenol or the surgical ablation of the cervical sympathetic chain may be considered. However, paradoxically this procedure may aggravate the patient's pain or result in new symptoms, such as compensatory and gustatory sweating.

MUSCLE SPASTICITY AND RELATED PHENOMENA

Severe muscle spasticity, spastic dystonia, flexor and extensor muscle spasms and associated limb reactions are common problems in patients with stroke. All of these phenomena or any combination of them may occur in the same patient.

Spastic dystonia is characterised by an increase in muscle tone that is present in the resting state. It results in abnormal postures, e.g. the characteristicly adducted, flexed and internally rotated posture of the upper limb or the equino-varus deformity of the foot in a hemiplegic patient. Flexor and extensor muscle spasms are sudden, usually painful, involuntary flexion or extension of the limbs that may or may not be accompanied by urinary and/or faecal incontinence. They are usually triggered by various stimuli, including touch, sudden noise or an attempt by the patient to execute a voluntary movement. Severe flexor and extensor spasms may cause difficulties with sitting safely in a chair or even lying in bed. The commonest, and probably the most clinically important phenomenon associated with spasticity is the associated reactions of the spastic upper limb in hemiplegic stroke patients.

Associated reactions of the paretic upper limb

In patients with upper motor neurone lesions a motor activity, especially if it involves excessive effort, frequently results in involuntary movements of one or more distant muscle groups. This phenomenon is known as associated reactions (ARs) and is closely related to muscle spasticity. ARs are sometimes referred to as associated movements. The term synkinesia is also used synonymously with ARs.

ARs of the paralysed upper limb occur in 80% of stroke patients. They are believed to be due to the release of postural reflexes from supra-spinal cortical control. The basic underlying mechanism responsible for the initial limb displacement was shown to be the reflex activation of the biceps brachii muscle. The brachioradialis does not seem to be implicated in this response.

ARs of the paralysed arm are characterised by sudden flexion at the elbow, abduction and elevation of the shoulder. They are usually triggered when the subject attempts to stand from a sitting position or when he initiates stepping. The involuntary movement may continue for several seconds after the event that triggered it had stopped. There is a marked variation between individuals in their response to stimuli that trigger the ARs. However, it appears that there is a direct correlation between the degree of the physical effort that is required to carry out the intended movement and the severity of the ARs. For example, a patient may have a normal gait when walking indoors but the challenge to postural stability during walking on an uneven terrain may result in the appearance of ARs. Although ARs usually occur when a voluntary movement is being attempted, they may also result from involuntary actions such as yawning, coughing or sneezing.

Severe ARs often impair motor function and usually require treatment. They accentuate the hemiplegic posture, interfere with balance reactions and compromise safe ambulation. Therapeutic interventions such as gait and balance training, usually require considerable effort by the hemiplegic patient in the early stages of recovery from stroke. This may aggravate the ARs and lead to abnormal postures.

The effects of spasticity
The increased muscle tone in patients with severe spasticity may result in impairment of voluntary movements. However, the relationship between the degree of hypertonia and the ability to perform a voluntary motor act in patients with pyramidal tract lesions is usually complex. In some patients spasticity does not appear to interfere significantly with motor function, while in others it restricts voluntary movements. An important requisite for efficient motor function is the relaxation of the antagonist muscle during the contraction of the prime mover. Failure of this reciprocal agonist/antagonist inhibition is sometimes observed in patients with spasticity. In these situations the successful treatment of spasticity often improves motor function. However, frequently the muscle weakness and the changes that occur in the contractile and visco-elastic properties of muscle in patients with longstanding spasticity are the main causes of the motor functional disability.

It should be remembered that spasticity is often functionally useful. It is usually invaluable for the maintenance of trunk posture, weight bearing on the weak lower limb and for ambulation. Other possible beneficial effects include the prevention of deep vein thrombosis in the paretic limb, and the maintenance of muscle mass and bone density. Therefore, the management of patients with spasticity should be based on a careful neurological examination and a detailed functional evaluation.

The principles of management of spasticity
The aim of management is to assess the severity of the impairments, to establish the extent of the functional disability, to define clearly the desired outcomes of treatment, to choose the most appropriate therapeutic interventions and the methods of monitoring their effects.

The decision to treat muscle spasticity should be based on a comprehensive functional assessment and clearly defined therapeutic goals. Ideally a multi-disciplinary team should carry out the assessment and set the treatment goals. Treatment goals must be realistic and meaningful to the individual and should be explained and agreed in advance with the patients and their carers. The choice of the therapeutic intervention in a given case depends on many factors. For example, the aim of treatment, the extent of the spasticity and the presence of other impairments and disabilities, the available resources and expertise etc. However, as a general rule, the use of different treatment modalities in combination results in greater symptomatic improvement and better functional outcomes than when only one type of intervention is used.

An individualised approach to the management of spasticity is essential. There is a large variation in the way muscle spasticity affects patients. The site and chronicity of the upper motor neurone lesion, its underlying cause, the degree of biological recovery and the way the individual compensates for the functional loss could explain the heterogeneity of the clinical manifestations of spasticity and its effects on motor function. To achieve optimal treatment outcomes in these circumstances it is important that an accurate analysis of the underlying abnormalities is made. This may sometimes require the use of investigations such as electromyography and instrumental gait analysis.

The indications for treatment
A common indication for treatment of muscle spasticity is to alleviate distressing symptoms, such as painful spasms. In some cases the aim is to improve motor function or to prevent or reduce the complications of muscle hypertonia including fixed contractures and joint dislocations. In patients with severe spasticity of the lower limb muscles the hypertonia often prevents comfortable and safe sitting in a chair or positioning in bed. Treatment of spasticity of the ankle plantar flexors is indicated in cases of dynamic foot equinus that result in difficulties with safe and energy efficient walking and spasticity that prevents the effective use of an ankle-foot orthosis. Treatment may also be considered when sustained ankle clonus interferes with ambulation by preventing the correct heel contact with the ground or when it causes difficulties with foot placement on the footplate of a wheelchair.

Several treatment modalities are used for the relief of muscle spasticity. These are antispasticity drugs, chemical neurolysis, botulinum toxin injections, physiotherapy, splinting and the use of plaster casts, cryotherapy, electrical stimulation and surgery.

General Measures
Empirical clinical observations suggest that many conditions, including urinary tract infections, pressure sores, faecal impaction, ingrown toe nails, and contractures may aggravate

muscle spasticity. These conditions should be routinely looked for in patients with stroke and, when present, appropriately managed.

Oral antispasticity drugs
The major oral antispasticity drugs are baclofen, the benzodiazepines, dantrolene and tizanidine. These drugs reduce muscle tone by different mechanisms and may be used in combination. Treatment with baclofen should be started with a small dose (e.g. 5mg tds). The dose is then titrated up over 2-3 weeks until the desired effect on spasticity is obtained. In most patients this can be achieved with a total daily dose of 60mg. Sudden withdrawal of baclofen after prolonged use is not advisable as it may precipitate serious complications, including epileptic seizures and hallucinations. Discontinuation of treatment with baclofen should be carried out gradually over at least 2 weeks.

Diazepam is a very potent antispasticity agent but doses of up to 60 mg/day may be required before a good clinical effect can be achieved. The use of the benzodiazepines for the treatment of spasticity is limited by their adverse effects which include sedation, amnesia and mental confusion. In addition, the prolonged use of these drugs in high doses is associated with the risk of drug dependence and depression. Paradoxically, the long-term use of diazepam may increase muscle spasticity, precipitate an anxiety state, aggression and insomnia.

Dantrolene is also an effective antispasticity drug with an adverse effect profile similar to that of baclofen. In addition, very rarely it can cause hepatic failure. The incidence of the hepatic adverse effects correlates with the dose of dantrolene and the duration of treatment. They seldom occur in patients receiving less than 400 mg/day (which is the maximum recommended dose) or in the first two months of treatment. It is recommended that liver function is measured before the commencement of treatment and at regular intervals thereafter.

Tizanidine has an antispasticity effect similar to that of baclofen and diazepam. It is claimed that tizanidine has the additional advantage of reducing muscle tone without causing muscle weakness and that it is particularly effective in younger patients and in those with very severe spasticity, especially when pain in the spastic muscle is a prominent feature. In most cases the optimal dose of tizanidine is 16 mg/day. Treatment is usually started with a small dose, e.g. 2mg daily. The dose is then increased gradually every third day until the desired effect on muscle tone is obtained. The main adverse effects of this drug are dose-dependent and include sedation, bradycardia and hypotension.

Large doses of oral antispasticity drugs often produce generalised muscle weakness. This is a major drawback, as the reduction of muscle strength may increase the functional disability in most patients, especially when trunk and other postural muscles are affected. Sometimes these drugs reduce muscle strength in the unaffected extremities without significantly reducing the spasticity or improving function of the spastic limbs. Furthermore, the value of oral antispasticity drugs diminishes with prolonged use. Tolerance develops after a few months of treatment, and incremental increases in dosage are often required to maintain the same clinical response. This usually increases the incidence and severity of the dose-dependent adverse effects of these drugs.

Chemical neurolysis
The destruction of peripheral nerves with phenol or alcohol (chemical neurolysis) is an effective method of treatment of localised muscle hypertonia. Chemical neurolysis can be achieved with peripheral nerve blocks or motor point injections, i.e. intramuscular injections of alcohol or phenol into the area of arborization of the motor nerve terminals. These procedures are generally safe, effective and relatively easy to perform in the outpatient clinic. They are claimed to have the benefit of relieving muscle spasticity without significantly weakening the strength of voluntary movements. The clinical effect on muscle spasticity is immediate because of the local anaesthetic properties of alcohol and phenol. This effect may last for several hours and is followed by recurrence of the hypertonia once the anaesthetic effect has worn off. Muscle denervation accounts for the more permanent effect of neurolysis and is maximal approximately 2-3 weeks after the injection.

In stroke patients chemical neurolysis of peripheral nerves is most frequently used for spasticity of the ankle plantar flexors and hip adductors. The neurolytic agent is injected into the medial popliteal nerve (MPN). The MPN can be easily localised with a nerve stimulator in the popliteal fossa at the level of the skin crease with the patient in the prone position and the leg fully extended. Alternatively, motor point injections can be carried out

133

as follows. The visible bulk of the calf muscles is divided into four quadrants and the middle of each quadrant is infiltrated with 1.5-2ml of the neurolytic agent. Motor point injections are less effective than nerve blocks in abolishing spasticity. Their beneficial effect on muscle tone is also shorter and lasts on average 4-6 weeks compared to more than three months in the case of nerve blocks. However, because the technique of motor point injections is simple and inexpensive, this procedure still has a place in the treatment of localised muscle spasticity, especially when the financial cost of treatment is an important consideration or when the necessary equipment or expertise to perform nerve blocks is not available. Obturator nerve blocks may be used to reduce hip adductor spasticity.

The optimal concentration of alcohol for peripheral nerve blocks and motor point injections has been shown to be 45%. (But 50% alcohol is usually used because it is easier to make up this concentration). Interestingly, the effect of 50% alcohol is comparable to that of 4.5% phenol and lasts 3-11 months with a mean duration of nearly five months. Phenol is less likely than alcohol to cause paraesthsiae and dysaesthesiae when used for chemical neurolysis of mixed sensory-motor nerves and may, therefore, be considered the drug of first choice for medial popliteal nerve blocks.

Complications of peripheral nerve blocks are rare. Painful dysaethesia and sensory loss in the foot may follow MPN blocks. Excessive weakening of the gastro-soleus muscle may also occur. This often interferes with walking because of the reduced "push off" in the preswing phase of the gait cycle. Local sepsis due to the injections is rare because of the antiseptic properties of alcohol and phenol. Occasionally a transient neuralgic type of pain develops in the dermatome of the injected nerve.

Botulinum toxin (Btx)
Btx is a potent neurotoxin that is produced by the anaerobic bacterium clostridium botulinum. There are seven known serotypes of Btx. Of these, type A (BtxA) is the most potent. The toxin blocks the release of acetylcholine at the neuromuscular junction. It also interferes with the function of cholinergic autonomic fibres. The clinical effect of BtxA on motor function is observed within a few days of an intramuscular injection and usually lasts 3-4 months. Restoration of neurotransmission starts with the formation of new synaptic connections with the intact neurones in the vicinity of the affected nerve terminals (collateral

sprouting) and is completed when recovery of the affected nerve terminals (regenerative sprouting) occurs.

Of the seven serotypes of Btx only type A and type B are commercially available at present. BtxA is marketed as Dysport (Ipsen Ltd) or Botox (Allergan, Inc). Identical quantities, unit for unit, of the two products differ in their clinical potency and have an approximate therapeutic equivalence ratio of three to one. The drug is presented as a toxin-haemagglutinin complex in powder form which is reconstituted in 0.9% sodium chloride solution. One vial of Dysport yields 500 units of the toxin. It is recommended that Dysport is reconstituted in 2.5 ml of normal saline to give 200 U/ml. A vial of Botox contains 100 units and is normally diluted in 1ml of normal saline. Currently the manufacturers of the BtxA recommend that the drug is discarded if not used within eight hours of its reconstitution. BtxB (NeuroBloc, Elan Pharma Ltd) is available as a ready made solution in doses of 5,000 and 10,000 units.

Btx is effective in the symptomatic relief of muscle spasticity. It can lead to improvement in the patients' disability and often reduces the amount of assistance with activities of daily living that is required by the patient. In stroke patients with a spastic, functionally useless upper limb treatment of the flexors of the elbow, wrist and fingers is often indicated. In these cases treatment may be necessary to improve access to the palm of the hand and the armpit for cleaning, and to enable the patients or their carers to put the spastic arm through sleeves of garments. Severe associated upper limb reactions of the paralysed arm may also be abolished or reduced with Btx injections into the biceps brachii and brachioradialis muscles. The muscles that are frequently injected in the upper limb are the biceps brachii, brachioradialis, pronator teres, flexor carpi ulnaris, flexor carpi radialis, flexor digitorum superficialis, flexor digitorum profundus and muscles of the thenar eminence. In the lower limbs the gastrosoleus muscle complex is injected to reverse dynamic foot equinus. Injection of the tibialis posterior muscle may be required when a varus deformity is also present. In most patients the optimal total dose of BtxA for upper limb spasticity is 1000 units of Dysport or 350 units of Botox (assuming a dose conversion ratio of 3:1). Half this dose is usually sufficient for the treatment of spasticity of the ankle plantar flexors.

Btx treatment is given by intramuscular injections. Accurate placement of the injection into the motor end plate zone (under

EMG guidance) is usually not necessary because the toxin readily diffuses in muscle and avidly binds to the nerve terminals at the neuromuscular junction. The use of surface anatomical landmarks to place the injection into the muscle belly is sufficient in most cases.

The antispasticity effect of Btx may be enhanced if it is combined with electrical stimulation (ES), physiotherapy or the use of booster injections. ES is thought to potentiate the effects of treatment with Btx on muscle tone by increasing the uptake of the toxin at the neuromuscular junction. The muscles may be stimulated using surface electrodes with a dual channel stimulator delivering 50-90 mA constant current pulses of 0.2 ms duration and 20 Hz frequency. Good results were reported using a protocol of 30-minute sessions of ES three times a day for the first 3 days after the Btx injection. Similarly, it was claimed that if physiotherapy is started in the first 24 hours after the Btx injection, it enhances the antispasticity effect of the toxin. The antispasticity effect of Btx may also be enhanced by the use of "booster injections", i.e. additional injections given within 2-3 weeks of the initial treatment. However, this strategy may increase the risk of Btx antibody formation and should be avoided.

Poor response to treatment with Btx may develop after an initial period of good clinical improvement. An important cause of this secondary treatment failure is the formation of neutralising Btx antibodies. This has been reported in 3 to 5% of patients who receive repeated treatments with BtxA. However, secondary treatment failure is more often due to other causes. These include poor injection techniques, insufficient dose, progression of the underlying disease or the presence of any of the factors that often aggravate muscle spasticity.

True unresponsiveness to Btx due to neutralising antibodies should be suspected when the toxin fails to induce muscle weakness or cause muscle atrophy and it can be confirmed with the in vivo mouse protection assay. However, this is an expensive test that is not readily available. An alternative is the eyebrow and frontalis muscle test. A small dose of BtxA (Dysport 40 IU or Botox 15 IU) is injected into the medial aspect of one eyebrow or into the frontalis muscle on one side. Preserved symmetry of eyebrow elevation or on frowning a few days after the injection suggests the presence of antibodies to BTxA.

Three factors are known to be associated with Btx antibody formation. These are a large cumulative dose of the toxin, a short time interval between treatments (less than three months), and the use of "booster" injections. Consequently, the measures that prevent or reduce the risk of developing Btx antibodies are: the use of the smallest effective dose of the drug, avoidance of booster injections and a longer time interval between successive treatments.

BtxA has a good safety profile. The common adverse effects of treatment include excessive weakness of the muscles adjacent to the site of the injection, flu-like symptoms, generalised fatigue (without overt muscle weakness), skin rashes, a dry mouth and dizziness. A few cases of brachial neuritis have also been reported. Mild orthostatic hypotension and subclinical abnormalities of heart rate and blood pressure responses to standing, physical exercise and Valsalva manoeuvre appear to be common in patients treated with BtxA. The severity of autonomic dysfunction is dose-dependent and usually lasts longer than the paralytic effects of BtxA on muscle. Occasionally the toxin spreads to muscles distant from the site of the injection. EMG and biopsy evidence of denervation without clinically detectable weakness has been shown to occur in these muscles following treatment with therapeutic doses of BtxA. However, the combination of overt and clinically significant paralysis of distant muscles and neurophysiological evidence of widespread muscle denervation has been reported in only a handful of patients to date. Nonetheless, treatment with BtxA should be carried out by a clinician who is familiar with this drug and patients receiving this treatment should be followed up on a regular basis.

Physiotherapy, the use of splints and plaster casts
Fixed contractures develop when the muscle fibre is maintained in a shortened state by immobilisation or by a continuous muscle contraction. Poor sitting postures and incorrect positioning of the patient in bed also predispose and aggravate fixed muscle contractures. Physiotherapy reduces the risk of developing fixed muscle contractures because regular muscle stretch reduces spasticity. Other methods of physiotherapy, such as strategies to improve the alignment of body segments and symmetry also contribute to tone reduction in the spastic muscles. Similarly, correct manual handling (e.g. during the patient's transfers from bed to chair etc.) and positioning of the patient in bed or chair are effective means of controlling the muscle hypertonia. Instruction of members of the rehabilitation team and the patient's carers on

the correct methods of manual handling and positioning of the patient is, therefore, an important aspect of the management of increased muscle tone.

The structure and visco-elastic properties of a muscle are altered when it is maintained in a shortened state by muscle hypertonia and/or immobility. The immobility and reduced range of motion in lower and upper limb joints (which are frequently associated with spasticity) also result in changes of the biochemical composition of the periarticular collagen. This combination of changes in the hypertonic muscle and the periarticular soft tissues usually leads to the development of fixed contractures. The use of splints and plaster casts prevents or delays this complication by preserving the optimal length of muscle and range of motion. These methods of treatment complement each other and may be used to treat established spasticity and/ or for the primary prevention of fixed contractures. The benefit of muscle stretching in the prevention of contractures appears to correlate with the duration and intensity of treatment.

The application of plaster casts is an effective treatment method in the short-term management of spasticity and is especially valuable when it is started early before the onset of contractures. The casts are applied with the limb positioned 5 to 10 degrees less than the joint range of motion that can be achieved on maximal passive muscle stretch. The plaster casts are replaced every 5-7 days using the same procedure each time. Care must be taken to protect the skin, especially in unconscious patients and in patients with skin sensory loss or aphasic patients who are not able to communicate their distress easily. The main disadvantage of plaster casts is that they limit the functional use of the limb and the immobilisation due to their use may cause disuse muscle atrophy. The application and subsequent replacements of the plaster casts are also time-consuming.

Cryotherapy
Cooling of muscle interferes with the peripheral components of the stretch reflex. It delays neuromuscular transmission and inhibits the excitability of the muscle spindle, but it also prolongs the muscle contraction. However, the net effect is usually reduction in muscle tone. The immersion of the spastic limb into cold water (t= 7º C) or the application of ice packs onto the muscle for 20 to 30 minutes usually results in noticeable reduction in the muscle tone. Clonus is abolished after 30 minutes of cooling. However, because this effect is usually modest, cryotherapy has limited

clinical value in the management of spasticity. Furthermore, its duration of effect on the spastic muscle is relatively short; usually lasting one hour after cooling had been discontinued. Consequently, this method of treatment is useful when a temporary reduction in spasticity is needed. For example, to facilitate a procedure such as the application of plaster casts or before physiotherapy. Paradoxically, in some patients cryotherapy may lead to marked increase in spasticity.

Functional electrical stimulation

Electrical stimulation of neural structures has been shown to reduce tone in spastic muscles, although the neurophysiological mechanisms that underlie this effect have not been fully elucidated. Clinical improvement in spasticity and reduction in painful muscle spasms may occur following spinal cord stimulation, transcutaneous electrical nerve stimulation and cerebellar stimulation.

Functional electrical stimulation (FES) has been shown to improve gait in hemiplegic stroke patients with a spastic foot drop. It is based on the principle that electrical stimulation can result in a contraction resulting in a functional movement of the paralysed muscle. Stimulation of the common peroneal nerve (CPN) of the paralysed leg is used to cause anlke dorsiflexion and foot clearance of the ground in the swing phase of the gait cycle. The CPN is stimulated by a skin surface electrode placed at the level of the head of the fibula. Another surface electrode is placed on the tibialis anterior muscle. The device is triggered by a foot switch placed under the heel. FES has no beneficial carry over effect once the nerve stimulation ceases.

DEEP VEIN THROMBOSIS

The patient's risk of developing lower limb deep vein thrombosis (DVT) is very high in the early period after stroke. Above knee DVT occurs in one in every five patients in the first month of stroke. The main factors that predispose to this complication are the flaccid muscle tone of the paralysed leg and the patient's reduced mobility. Prevention of DVT is, therefore, an important part of the early management of stroke. The main strategies for the prevention of DVT after stroke are treatment with heparin, the use of compression stockings and early mobilisation of the patient.

Low doses of heparin administered subcutaneously are sometimes used for the prophylaxis of DVT in patients with reduced mobility, e.g. after surgery. However, this treatment should be avoided in stroke patients because of the risk of intracerebral haemorrhage or the haemorrhagic transformation of an infarct. This risk probably outweighs any potential benefit in most patients. The secondary prevention of stroke with antithrombotic agents has been shown to reduce the occurrence of DVT and pulmonary thrombo-embolism. In practice the combined use of antithrombotic agents (for the secondary prevention of ischaemic stroke) with compression thromboembolism deterrent (TED) stockings is probably sufficient for the prevention of DVT after stroke.

Compression TED stockings are effective in the prevention of DVT in the peri-operative period in immobile surgical patients and a similar effect is also likely in bed ridden non-surgical patients. They are widely used in the early stage of stroke and are thought to reduce the risk of DVT by reducing venous stasis and improving the venous blood flow in the paralytic limb. Full-length stockings are probably preferable to below knee stocking, but they are usually less well tolerated by patients and are more likely to be soiled if the patient is incontinent of urine or faeces. Compression stockings should be used until the patient's mobility has improved. They should be avoided in patients with peripheral vascular disease and in those with sensory peripheral neuropathy, as they may cause skin necrosis.

Lower limb DVT may develop despite the use of the above measures. Its main clinical features are: localised swelling, pain and tenderness of the affected limb. Redness and heat of the overlying skin may also be present. Sometimes the patient may develop symptoms and signs of pulmonary embolism in the absence of obvious signs of lower limb DVT. Measurement of D-dimer blood levels is a useful initial screening test for DVT (D-dimer is a protein that is formed as a result of degradation of a thrombus). A positive D-dimer test, especially if a sensitive assay method, such ELISA, is used suggests the presence of DVT. The diagnosis may then be confirmed with Doppler ultrasound studies, venography or a magnetic resonance imaging (MRI) scan.

Stroke patients with confirmed DVT require anticoagulation, initially with heparin and an oral anticoagulant, followed by oral anticoagulation alone. Warfarin is the drug of first choice for the long-term treatment of DVT. The dose is titrated to give an international normalised ratio (INR) of between 2 and 3. Treatment should be given for 3 months in patients with uncomplicated lower limb DVT, but a total of 6 months is recommended for those who develop pulmonary embolism. Insertion of a filter into the inferior vena cava may be considered in patients with DVT in whom the use of warfarin is contra indicated and in those who develop pulmonary embolism whilst on optimal anticoagulant therapy.

THALAMIC PAIN

Thalamic stroke is relatively common, occurring in about 20% of all cerebrovascular events. Fortunately, only a small proportion of stroke patients develop thalamic pain. This complication usually follows strokes affecting the ventral intermediate and ventral caudal nuclei of the thalamus and often constitutes part of Dejerine-Roussy syndrome (D-RS). In addition to the characteristic pain, patients with D-RS present with motor weakness (which is usually mild), transient hemianopia and hemisensory loss. The impairment of sensory function is frequently severe and chronic, lasting many years. Upper and lower limb dystonia and other involuntary movements may also be present. As a rule post-stroke thalamic pain starts days or weeks after the vascular event and may persist for years. It is usually severe and is often described as burning. Depression is common in patients with thalamic pain.

Thalamic pain is often resistant to treatment with analgesics, antidepressants and anticonvulsants. In recent years chronic electrical stimulation of the motor cortex has been reported to be effective.

Dysaesthesia and hyperaesthesia of the affected half of the body may also occur after stroke. These symptoms are usually transient and do not require specific treatment. However, in severe cases carbamazepine is usually effective.

FURTHER READING

Dysphagia

Crockford C, Smithard DG. The swallow test. *Royal College of Speech & Language Therapists Bulletin*; 1997: 7-9

Collins MJ, Bakheit AMO. Does pulse oximetry reliably detect aspiration in dysphagic stroke patients? *Stroke* 1997; **28**:1773-1775

Park RHR, Allison MC, Lang J, 0 et al. Randomised comparison of percutaneous endoscopic gastrostomy and nasogastric tube feeding in patients with persisting neurological dysphagia. *British Medical Journal* 1993; **304**: 1406-1409

Schneider I, Thumfart WF, Potoschnig C, Eckel HE. Treatment of dysfunction of the cricopharyngeal muscle with botulinum A toxin: introduction of a new non-invasive method. *Annals of Otology, Rhinology & Laryngology* 1994,**103**:31-35

Mood disorders

Singh A, Hermann N, Black SE. The importance of lesion location in poststroke depression: a critical review. *Canadian Journal of Psychiatry* 1998; **43**: 921-927

Ross ED, Rush AJ. Diagnosis and neuroanatomical correlates of depression in brain damaged patients. *Archives of General Psychiatry* 1981; **38**: 1344-1354

Chemerinski E, Robinson RG, Kosier JT. Improved recovery in activities of daily living associated with remission of poststroke depression. *Stroke* 2001; **32**: 113-117

Gill D, Hatcher S. Antidepressants for depression in medical illness. Cochrane Database of Systemic Reviews 2000, 2: CD001312

Shoulder pain

Anonymous. Need patients be stuck with frozen shoulder? *Drug & Therapeutics Bulletin* 2000; **38**: 86-88

Turner-Stokes L, Jackson D. Shoulder pain after stroke: a review of the evidence base to inform the development of an integrated care pathway. *Clinical Rehabilitation* 2002; **16**: 276-298

Price CM, Pandyan AD. Electric stimulation for preventing and treating post-stroke shoulder pain (Cochrane Review). In: The Cochrane Library 1999, Issue 4. Oxford: Update Software, 199

Geurts ACH, Visschers BAJT, van Limbeek J, Ribbers GM. Systematic review of aetiology and treatment of post-stroke hand oedema and shoulder hand syndrome. *Scandinavian Journal of Rehabilitation Medicine* 2000; **32**: 4-10

Muscle spasticity

Barnes MP, Johnson GR (eds). *Upper motor neurone syndrome and spasticity. Clinical management and neurophysiology.* Cambridge University Press, Cambridge, 2001

Bakheit A M O. *Botulinum toxin treatment of muscle spasticity.* 2nd edition, Authorhouse, Milton Keynes, 2007

CHAPTER FIVE

RHABILITATION OF STROKE PATIENTS

Complete neurological and functional recovery is rare after severe stroke. In addition, most stroke patients are frail elderly subjects who often have other chronic diseases, such as degenerative arthritis or ischaemic heart disease. The onset of stroke may aggravate the age-related decline in the physical and cognitive competencies of these patients and also adds to the disability due to the pre-existing chronic disease. Consequently, older patients with moderately severe or severe stroke usually require lengthy rehabilitation initially in hospital and, later, in the community. Both the environment in which stroke care is delivered, and the process of care are important for achieving optimal clinical outcomes.

THE ORGANISATION OF STROKE CARE
There is now extensive evidence that management of stroke patients in specialist stroke units reduces mortality and morbidity, improves the functional outcomes for patients and reduces the length of the patient's stay in hospital. Therefore, ideally all stroke patients who require hospitalisation should be admitted to a stroke unit. Those with mild stroke or transient ischaemic attacks should have rapid access to specialist stroke services, for example a neurovascular clinic for the rapid assessment and initiation of measures to reduce the risk of a further stroke, or to out-patient hospital care or domiciliary rehabilitation, as required.

A stroke unit may be defined as an in-patient clinical facility that is designated exclusively for the treatment and rehabilitation of stroke patients, and in which care is delivered by a multidisciplinary team of healthcare professionals with knowledge and expertise in stroke. Although there is a general agreement on this definition, there are different models of delivery of specialist stroke care.

The main models of stroke units in the UK are acute stroke units and integrated acute and rehabilitation stroke units. In some hospitals patients are initially admitted to a stroke intensive care unit and then transferred to an acute stroke unit for a few days until they are fully investigated and received acute medical treatment, e.g. thrombolysis. Once they are medically stable they are discharged to a separate rehabilitation unit. By contrast, patients who are admitted to an integrated acute stroke and rehabilitation unit are managed by the same team throughout their hospital stay. The latter is probably a better and more cost-effective model of delivery of specialist stroke care. Irrespective of the model of care used, most stroke services also have outpatient rehabilitation units, as well as community stroke rehabilitation teams. The community stroke teams support patients at home and, thus, enable early discharge from hospital. They usually operate from a hospital base and work closely with the stroke unit.

THE PROCESS OF CARE

Although individual therapy interventions are important for promoting recovery after stroke, it is generally recognised that the quality of the overall rehabilitation programme is what determines the final functional outcome for the patient. In addition to delivering the appropriate remedial therapies, the rehabilitation programme should aim to utilise the patient's positive personal attributes and to take into account the physical environment to which he will return following discharge from hospital. It should also recognise the potential long-term benefits of enabling him to maintain contact with his social network.

The rehabilitation programme should be a coordinated multidisciplinary team (MDT) activity that is based on explicitly agreed treatment goals. The process should start with an assessment of the patient's impairments, the resulting limitations in functional activities (i.e. the disabilities) and their impact on social participation. It is also important to know about the patient's personal attributes and the physical environmental and social factors that might act as assets or barriers to successful rehabilitation and the patient's ability to maintain functional independence after discharge from hospital. This assessment is then used for setting the treatment goals and also as a baseline for monitoring the patient's response to the rehabilitation programme. Rehabilitation is an educational process and it is important to explain to the patients and their carers the common features of stroke, how these might affect them and what is the best way to overcome the difficulties arising from them. The MDT should monitor the patient's progress and review the therapy plan periodically, usually once or twice a week. It should also start early to plan the patient's discharge from hospital and to arrange the post-discharge follow up and support in the community. The rehabilitation care plan is summarised in the diagram below.

Figure 5.1
The main stages in the rehabilitation process

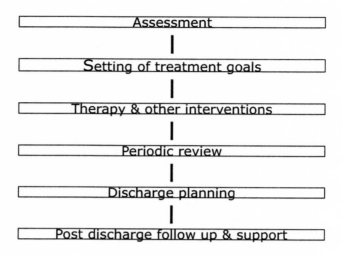

Assessment of the impairments and their consequences
The main physical impairments after stroke are muscle weakness, reduction or loss of skin sensation, visual field deficits, dysphagia, dysphasia, dysarthria, dyspraxia, unilateral hemispatial neglect, poor balance and impairment of cognitive function. The methods of assessment of these impairments are described in chapters three and four. It is important that every member of the stroke rehabilitation team, irrespective of their specialty, has a good working knowledge of these symptoms and their possible effects on the patient's health and functional abilities. This is because the successful management of most of these impairments and their functional consequences usually requires input from different members of staff and the contribution of each of them should be consistent and in accordance with the agreed overall therapy plan. For example, if a decision to manage unilateral hemispatial neglect with impairment training, rather than task specific training (see chapter three) is made, then all team members should adopt the same strategy in all their dealings with the patient. For instance, the patient should be approached from the affected side and visual, tactile or auditory cues are used to direct his attention to the neglected hemispace when given medication by the nurse, during physiotherapy, or while undergoing training for independence with washing and dressing by the occupational therapist. Even the patient's family members and visitors can

be involved in the patient's rehabilitation by adopting the same approach.

Setting of the rehabilitation goals
A coordinated, goal-directed teamwork is the corner stone of the management of stroke patients and is probably one of the main reasons for the reported better clinical recovery of patients treated in stroke units compared to those who receive treatment in general medical wards. A well-led multidisciplinary team (MDT) has unity of purpose, avoids duplication of effort by individual team members, delivers organised care, rather than random treatments, and focuses on improving the patient's functional abilities. Setting of the treatment goals is central to effective teamwork. It helps to direct the MDT activity, to motivate the patient and staff and to enable a meaningful monitoring of the patient's improvement (or deterioration) over time against expected recovery milestones.

Treatment goals are the functional and social outcomes desired by the patient and expected to result from the rehabilitation process. They should not be confused with therapy goals which are the actions required to direct the therapeutic and other rehabilitative interventions. For example, the treatment goal of a hemiplegic patient may be to be able to walk short distances indoors by the time of discharge from hospital. The therapy goals relevant to this could include a series of actions of progressively increasing complexity, such as training the patient to regain his balance in sitting and standing, then to stand and practice stepping with the therapists and then to walk on the ward with assistance, then with supervision only, etc.

The process of setting appropriate treatment goals is complex. The MDT needs to analyse the patient's impairments and their functional consequences for the patient and his carers, and to have a good knowledge of the likely course and prognosis of the underlying disease. In order to set realistic treatment goals it is also important to consider the patient's previous level of functioning, co morbidities and general health and to ascertain the patient's wishes.

A patient's cooperation and motivation for a given treatment goal is likely to be influenced by his personal interest in that objective (i.e. the desired outcome of treatment) and the effort required to achieve it. The expectations of the MDT (which are usually based on their perception of the patient's needs) should not be the basis for setting the treatment goals because what is important to the professional staff might not be important to the patient. Therapy goals should, therefore, be negotiated, and not imposed.

The acronym SMART (which refers to sensible, measurable, achievable, relevant and time-limited) is an easy to remember description of a properly set treatment goal. A sensible goal is a realistic one that takes into account the severity of the patient's impairments and previous functional abilities. It is neither too ambitious, nor too easy and is likely to be achieved with the appropriate therapeutic intervention and effort by the patient. Goal setting should be a dynamic process because patients' needs (and their perceptions of needs) and wishes may change over time.

The therapy and other interventions for stroke
The therapeutic interventions for stroke aim:
1. To reduce disability by managing the impairments and, through independence training, to compensate for the effects of loss of function and to enable the acquisition of new functional skills.
2. To mitigate the impact of disability by the use of technology and environmental adaptations.
3. To optimise the patient's functional abilities at crisis points, e.g. functional deterioration after an acute infection or a fall.
4. To prevent or treat complications, such as severe muscle spasticity.

Review of the patient's response to rehabilitation
The purpose of rehabilitation following stroke is to help patients recover lost function, or to develop optimal skills to compensate for the functional loss, and also to facilitate their emotional adjustment to the resulting residual disability and its impact on social participation and quality of life. Rehabilitation is considered successful when it enables the patient to achieve functional independence in mobility and activities of daily living (ADL) and to resume previous family and social roles, including return to gainful employment and leisure activities. Therefore, monitoring of the patient's response to rehabilitation should be based on functional outcome measures.

In routine clinical practice the use of a goal attainment scale and a simple global functional scale, e.g. the Barthel index of activities of daily living, is usually sufficient. Goal attainment scales are particularly valuable because they can be adapted to the goals of the individual patient (rather than the perception of their carers and the rehabilitation professionals). When seemingly realistic goals are not met, an attempt should be made to establish and rectify the cause of this failure. Common barriers to effective rehabilitation after stroke include anxiety and depression and subclinical intercurrent illness, such as asymptomatic urinary tract infection.

Planning discharge from hospital
Most patients who survive stroke wish to live at home after the initial episode of care in hospital. Enabling patients to return to live in their own homes is a worthwhile aim of rehabilitation and should be pursued, whenever possible. Return to live at home has several benefits. It helps to preserve the patients' self–identity in the face of poor health, loss of social roles and dependency. It also gives disabled individuals a sense of autonomy and control of their destiny and possibly motivates them to maintain their functional abilities. However, these advantages need to be weighed carefully against the possible risks of an unsafe home discharge. In addition to this risk assessment, due consideration should be given to the need for adaptations to the patient's home environment, the provision of therapy after discharge, if needed, and the practical and emotional support for patients and their carers.

The timely discharge of the patient from hospital is particularly important. Prolonged and unnecessary hospitalisation fosters functional dependency and may expose the patient to health risks, such hospital-acquired infection. Similarly, premature discharge, especially in the absence of adequate formal and informal social support and community rehabilitation services, may lead to loss of the skills acquired during the in-patient rehabilitation and may trigger avoidable re-admission to hospital or to institutional care. There is a large variation between individuals in the degree of functional independence that they need to achieve before they are fit for discharge from hospital. Nonetheless, adequate cognitive function, especially memory and safety judgement, and some independence with mobility and the ability to communicate with others effectively (e.g. to summon help in an emergency) are essential for patients who intend to live alone after they leave the hospital. The use of arbitrarily chosen criteria, such as the length of hospital stay or a predetermined score on the Barthel index of activities of daily living, is usually unhelpful and the timing of discharge from hospital should be considered on a case-by-case basis.

When planning the patient's discharge from hospital the MDT should take into account the wishes of the patients and their families, the severity of functional dependency, the suitability and safety of the environment in which the patient will live and the level of the available formal and informal social support.

Environmental adaptations – minor or major adaptations to the patient's home are often required before discharge from hospital even when the residual disability is relatively small. Learned motor tasks, such as walking, are automatic activities and their performance normally requires minimal conscious effort by the individual. However, with impairment of perceptual and cognitive function, or even just physical or mental fatigue, more attentional effort is usually needed to perform these activities safely, despite the relatively preserved motor function. For example, a person with unilateral hemispatial neglect and very mild hemiparesis may trip over minor obstacles, such as a loose rug, and fall when walking unless he concentrates his attention. A pre-discharge assessment of the patient in his own home should reveal such hazards. Sometimes the provision of equipment and aids is also necessary, but care should be taken to avoid provision of unnecessary aids and adaptations which are often powerful reminders of lost competencies and stigma.

Support for informal carers — informal social support in the context of healthcare is defined as the emotional, practical and informational help given to patients by their family members and friends. It is different from the interventions that are provided by health and social care professionals as part of their statutory duties.

Empathy, expressing concern, showing affection and giving reassurance are the main forms of emotional support. Emotional support appears to be more important than informational and practical support in the early stages of recovery from stroke. It has been shown to reduce depressive symptoms, improve the patient's self-esteem, promote adjustment to functional loss and protect against future maladaptive behaviour. Faster and more sustained recovery is usually seen in stroke patients who have wide social support networks and the extent of benefit is normally proportional to the amount of support given. Interestingly, supportive behaviour is most useful when it is considered by the patients to meet their needs.

In contrast to emotional support, practical social support is most beneficial when given in moderate amounts. It is important to realise that overprotective behaviour may foster functional dependency, encourage learned helplessness and increase reliance on others. On the other hand, inadequate practical support may lead to loss of functional gains following discharge from hospital.

Several reasons motivate people to become informal caregivers, including a sense of duty or loyalty and social pressure arising from other people's expectation. Carers are a valuable resource. Their contribution should be recognised and they should be offered practical and emotional support to reduce the stress associated with the physical demands and financial consequences of caring and the social restrictions imposed by caring.

Follow-up after discharge from hospital
Most stroke patients will need to attend out patient clinics periodically after discharge from hospital. The purpose of out patient clinic follow up is to monitor the patient's neurological and functional recovery, to anticipate and prevent loss of functional independence, to ensure that all modifiable stroke risk factors are optimally controlled, and to prevent secondary disability, e.g. by the timely management of severe muscle spasticity. In addition, frequently, patients experience significant emotional problems on return to their homes mainly due to changes in their family and social roles. As these patients often require professional help to adjust better to their new disability and its social consequences, monitoring of their emotional state and coping mechanisms after discharge from hospital is an important function of the out patient clinic. Clinic follow up also provides the opportunity to review the adequacy of the social support to the patient and his carers that was provided at the time of discharge home and to provide timely interventions, if necessary.

THE MAIN REHABILITATION THERAPY INTERVENTIONS
Although several mechanisms mediate the functional recovery after brain damage, in stroke unmasking and substitution appear to be the most important in the short and medium term (see chapter 2). These mechanisms are enhanced by goal-directed, task-specific training and are maintained by reinforcement, i.e. task repetition. The acquisition of new motor and cognitive skills

during rehabilitation is therefore influenced by the treatment intensity and the nature of the task (e.g. passive stimulation versus specific therapy). This is the basis for the therapy interventions in neurological rehabilitation.

The main therapeutic interventions used in the rehabilitation of stroke patients are physiotherapy, occupational therapy, speech and language therapy and cognitive therapy. Although treatment is typically delivered in time-limited therapy sessions, it is important to emphasise that it should be continued on the ward by the nursing and other staff to enable further practice and consolidation of the newly acquired skills. In this way the task-specific improvements in motor and other functions are incorporated into the patient's activities of daily living.

Physiotherapy
The aim of physiotherapy in stroke is to optimise the patient's motor functional recovery and to prevent the complications of poor postures, muscle hypertonia and immobility. Most stroke patients have sensory, perceptual and cognitive deficits in addition to the motor impairments and strategies to address these deficits should be incorporated in the physiotherapy programme. For example, the treatment of a patient with clinically significant unilateral hemispatial neglect should include specific instructions to improve spatial awareness during mobilisation and other motor functional activities.

Different treatment approaches that utilise muscle stretching and strengthening exercises and training to improve alignment of body parts, mobility and gait are used by physiotherapists. These therapeutic approaches include the Neurodevelopmental (Bobath) Method, the Proprioceptive Neuromuscular Facilitation technique, the Motor Re-learning Programme, the Orthopaedic approach, Constraint-induced Movement Therapy and Biofeedback therapy (see table 5.1). Analysis of the published evidence suggests that, on the whole, goal-directed therapy programmes that are directed at specific motor functions result in better clinical outcomes and shorter hospitalisation of patients than the impairment-focused therapy interventions, such as the Bobath method. In practice rarely one method of physiotherapy is used exclusively and, as a rule, the different physiotherapy methods or some of the component parts of these methods are utilised in combination in the treatment of the same patient.

Table 5.1
Description of the commonly used physiotherapy interventions in stroke

Physiotherapy method	Description
Neurodevelopmental Therapy (Bobath treatment)	Is based on techniques that inhibit abnormal postures and muscle hypertonia in order to restore normal movement patterns. The therapy puts more emphasis on the preparation and facilitation of the different components of movement than on task-specific activities.
Proprioceptive Neuromuscular Facilitation	Mainly used to increase the joints' range of motion through stimulation of the proprioceptors. It is also combined with isotonic and isometric exercises to strengthen weak muscles.
Motor Relearning Programme	Consists of active context-specific and task-specific practice (directed by the therapist), reinforcement and regular feedback.
The Orthopaedic Approach	The emphasis of this method is on enabling the patient to compensate for lost motor function by concentrating on muscle strengthening exercises and mobilisation of the affected and non-affected limbs.

Occupational therapy
Training patients to regain functional independence with activities of daily living (ADL), such as personal care, meal preparation, money management etc, is one of the main objectives of occupational therapy. In addition, occupational therapists

(OTs) contribute to the patient's overall clinical assessment by identifying the impact of any existing perceptual and cognitive deficits on the patient's performance of ADL. OTs also have an important role in planning the patient's discharge from hospital, including the pre-discharge assessment of the patient's functional abilities in his own environment, advice on home adaptations and home care, provision of equipment to aid or enhance functional independence, and assessment for return to employment and resumption of leisure activities.

Cognitive rehabilitation
Stroke may affect all domains of cognitive function, including mood, memory, attention, problem-solving ability and other executive function. Although spontaneous significant improvement or even complete recovery of cognitive abilities occurs in some cases, the symptoms persist in most stroke patients. Attentional deficits tend to improve better and faster than other cognitive impairments. By contrast, the prognosis of memory impairment is usually poor.

Post-stroke cognitive impairment requires treatment because it often interferes with successful rehabilitation and leads to poor clinical outcomes. It is also a strong predictor of deterioration of the patient's mobility and functional independence after discharge from hospital. Cognitive rehabilitation has been shown to be effective after stroke, especially for unilateral hemispatial neglect, dyspraxia, dysphasia (see chapter three), and mild to moderately severe memory impairment.

The main cognitive interventions for the treatment of memory impairment are memory training and the use of strategies to compensate for the poor memory. Patients should be helped to establish and adhere to a daily routine and changes to their physical environment should be avoided. This is because tasks and behaviours that are performed regularly and in the same context require little cognitive capacity, especially working memory and speed of cognitive processing. This strategy could be further supported by the use of memory aids, such as note taking.

The disability associated with stroke usually results in changes in the patient's personal relationships, life style, social and family roles and financial responsibilities. Consequently, depression, low self-esteem and poor adjustment to disability are common after stroke and often require treatment with antidepressant medication and/ or cognitive behavioural therapy (see chapter four).

REHABILITATION IN THE COMMUNITY
The provision of emotional and practical support for patients and their carers, especially during the transition from hospital to the community, is an important aspect of the rehabilitation programme. Many patients and their carers feel apprehensive about discharge from the safety of the hospital environment to their homes. Fear of another stroke, uncertainties about one's ability to cope at home, concerns about long term dependency and the need to adjust to new family and social roles and a sense of financial insecurity are common. These issues need to be addressed by the MDT. Reassurance, advice on benefits, employment, leisure activities, driving a motor vehicle and information about the community services provided by statutory and voluntary organisations are often required. Most patients will also need further therapeutic interventions in the community, including vocational rehabilitation.

Vocational rehabilitation
Return to gainful employment after stroke is an important goal of rehabilitation, even when severe disability persists. The income from employment often secures the individual's financial independence. In addition, people in paid work usually perceive themselves as valued members of society. This fosters a belief of self-worth and often enhances self-esteem. Other possible benefits of employment include the opportunity for social contacts and meaningful, structured time occupation. Long-term unemployment frequently results in financial dependency (on the State or on family members) and is associated with low mood and poor self-esteem. All of these factors may lead to social isolation. Stroke patients who are not of retirement age should therefore be encouraged to return to work.

The initial assessment for return to work is usually started in the hospital's occupational therapy department. This should preferably be followed by the direct observation of the patient's performance in the work place. Liaison at an early stage with the occupational health team of the patient's employers is essential. The aim of this assessment is to establish the patient's ability attend for work reliably, his behaviour in the work place, including his interaction with work colleagues and customers, his productivity, the impact of fatigue on performance and the need for supervision or practical support. The assessment should also include whether adaptations to the work environment would be necessary. In addition to the information derived from this assessment, the employer should also be advised on whether the patient has any residual disability, its nature and prognosis and the need for on-going therapy. In complex cases the advice of a qualified and experienced occupational health physician may be necessary.

When vocational rehabilitation is required it is best delivered through an employer-based programme, whenever possible. In some cases graded return to work may be necessary. Some patients may be able to do only flexible hours, part-time work or work from home and this needs to be negotiated with employers, either directly or through a statutory organisation, such as the Disability Advisory Service.

Supported employment and sheltered employment schemes, i.e. work in non-industrial settings, may be considered, if the patient is not able to do his previous job or an alternative, perhaps less demanding, work in the competitive market.

Driving a motor vehicle
Being able to drive a motor vehicle is necessary for most people in order to become independently mobile outside their home environment. Driving is particularly important for those with disabilities who live in geographically isolated rural areas that have no, or limited, public transport. This is why many stroke patients seek advice from medical staff on when they may resume driving a motor car after the cerebrovascular event.

In the UK driving licences are issued by the Driving and Vehicle Licensing Agency (DVLA). The DVLA also has the right to revoke a driving licence in certain circumstances, e.g. if the driver develops a new disability that makes driving unsafe or if an existing disability worsens to the extent that the subject is unable to continue to drive a motor car safely. The current legislation in the UK does not require doctors and other healthcare professionals to report the patient's lack of fitness to drive to the DVLA, but the medical staff have a duty of care to advise the patient to do so. The onus is on the drivers to inform the DVLA of any change in their health that might affect their fitness to drive. In the context of stroke, an exception to this rule is when the patient has recovered fully (defined here as having no residual neurological deficit) in the first month from the stroke onset. It is mandatory for the patient to inform the DVLA if complete recovery has not occurred within this time period.

All patients with a stroke or a transient ischaemic attack are barred from driving a motor vehicle for at least a month. If recovery is satisfactory after the first month of stroke, the patient may resume driving a motor car or a motor cycle (group 1 licences) provided that they did not have epileptic seizures as a result of the stroke. (Epileptic seizures in the first 24 hours after stroke are classified as provoked seizures. Patients with provoked seizures are assessed for fitness to drive by the DVLA on an individual basis). Holders of group 2 licences (Large Goods Vehicles and Passenger-Carrying Vehicles) have to fulfil more stringent criteria and should apply to the DVLA. Patients with recurrent TIAs over a short period of time should also notify the DVLA and they are normally required to give up driving until they are free of TIAs for at least three months.

The common impairments and disabilities after stroke that often interfere with the ability to drive a motor car safely are epilepsy, cognitive and perceptual impairment, severe aphasia, hemispatial neglect, visual field loss and severe limb weakness. These factors interfere with safe driving and should be thoroughly evaluated during the driving assessment. They often slow the speed of cognitive processing and increase the response reaction time, cause the driver to respond inappropriately to driving conditions or to experience difficulties with navigation. In some cases, on-the-road driving assessment may be necessary. Most regions in the UK have specialised driving assessment centres for people with disability.

Subjects who are deemed fit to drive after stroke may still experience difficulties, especially in challenging driving situations, e.g. during rush hour traffic, or while driving at night. Patients should be advised to avoid these situations and to plan their journeys in advance if travelling to unfamiliar areas. In some cases vehicle adaptations may be necessary.

Resumption of sexual intercourse after stroke
Sexual dysfunction is common after stroke. Hypersexuality may result from stroke in the thalamus or temporal lobe, but it is rare. Most men with post-stroke sexual dysfunction report a reduced libido and failure to produce or maintain penile erections. Female patients often complain of reduced vaginal lubrication and an inability to achieve orgasm. Coital frequency usually declines after stroke and dissatisfaction with sexual activity is common in both sexes.

The reasons for reduced sexual function after stroke are varied and include physical and psychological factors. Frequently, more than one factor is present in the same patient. As expected, advanced age, severe disability and possibly depression correlate with the decline in sexual activity after stroke. Fear of stroke recurrence is by far the most frequently cited reason by patients and their sexual partners for withdrawing from sexual intercourse.

The management of post-stroke sexual dysfunction should include psychotherapy or counselling. Drug treatment is also frequently required. Phosphodiesterase type −5 inhibitors, such as sildenafil (Viagra), is an effective treatment for erectile impotence and is safe in subjects without significant cardiovascular disease. The risk of stroke recurrence as a direct result of sildenafil administration appears to be very low if treatment is avoided in patients with symptomatic coronary heart disease and in those on multiple antihypertensive drugs. Sildenafil is contra indicated in patients on nitrates. It is recommended that sildenafil should not be used in the first six months after stroke.

Leisure activities
Hobbies and other leisure pursuits are pleasurable activities to the individual. They alleviate boredom and enable people to use their spare time in a way that is meaningful to them. Furthermore, they often provide opportunities for socialisation and friendships. Some leisure pursuits, especially outdoor activities, may also have additional health benefits. An important goal of rehabilitation is to help patients to occupy their spare time and to enable them to pursue their previous hobbies and lesisure activities or to develop new ones. Numerous voluntary organisations in the UK provide leisure facilititis and organise leisure activities for people with disabilities of all ages.

The role of social services and voluntary organisations
Patients with stroke are often socially isolated. Many factors may contribute to this, including the loss of physical independence, depression, poor motivation, low self-esteem and financial difficulties. In the UK social services departments of Local Authorities and many voluntary organisations offer services for stroke patients and their carers in "Day Centres", "Stroke Clubs" and supported employment schemes. These services provide emotional and practical support to patients and their families and, in addition, they help to reduce their social isolation.

RECOMMENDED FURTHER READING

Physiotherapy
Bobath B. *Adult hemiplegia: evaluation and treatment.* 2d edition. Butterworth-Heinmann, 1990
Carr JH, Shepherd RB. *A motor relearning programme for stroke.* Butterworth-Heinmann Physiotherapy, 1987
Chan DYL, Chan CCH, Au DKS. Motor relearning programme for stroke patients: a randomized controlled trial. *Clinical Rehabilitation* 2006; **20**: 191-200
Van Peppen RPS, Kwakkel G, Wood-Dauphinee S, Hendriks HJM, Van der Wees PhJ, Dekker J. the impact of physical therapy on functional outcomes after stroke: what's the evidence? *Clinical Rehabilitation* 2004; **18**: 833-862
Pollock AS, Baer G, Pomeroy V, Langhorne P. Physiotherapy treatment approaches for recovery of postural control and lower limb function following stroke. *Cochrane Database of Systematic Reviews* 2003; **2**: CD001920

Social support
Glass TA, Maddox GL. The quality and quantity of social support: stroke recovery as psycho-social transition. *Social Science Medicine* 1992; **34** : 1249-61

Cognitive rehabilitation
Van de Port IG, Kwakkel G, van Wijk I, Lindeman E. Susceptibility to deterioration of mobility long-term after stroke: a prospective cohort study. *Stroke* 2006; **37**: 167-171
Hochstenbach JB, den Otter R, Mulder TW. Cognitive recovery after stroke: a 2-year follow up. *Archives of Physical Medicine & Rehabilitation* 2003; **84**: 1499-1504
Cicerone KD, Dahlberg C, Malec JF, et al. Evidence-based cognitive rehabilitation: updated review of the literature from 1998 through 2002. *Archives of Physical Medicine & Rehabilitation* 2005; **86**: 1681-1692

CHAPTER SIX

THE SECONDARY PREVENTION OF STROKE

A patient who has had a stroke or TIA is at risk of having another one in the future. The chance of recurrence is approximately 5-8% per year and one in every six patients will have another stroke within 5 years of the index cerebrovascular event. The risk is higher in those with a haemorrhagic stroke. The overall management of stroke patients should therefore include the secondary prevention of stroke, i.e. a strategy to reduce the risk of stroke recurrence. The cornerstone of the secondary prevention of stroke caused by intracerebral haemorrhage is the optimal and sustained control of a raised blood pressure (BP) and the appropriate treatment of any underlying causes, such as an arteriovenous malformation. In those with an ischaemic stroke the preventative measures consist of the aggressive treatment of all modifiable stroke risk factors, the use of antithrombotic therapy and surgical interventions, where appropriate.

MANAGEMENT OF STROKE RISK FACTORS
Assessment for stroke risk factors is an important part of the initial management in the acute phase of stroke. This will enable the timely initiation of the appropriate measures to prevent stroke recurrence. The main potentially modifiable stroke risk factors should be sought and treated. These are hypertension, diabetes mellitus, atrial fibrillation, hyperlipidaemia, significant carotid artery stenosis and cigarette smoking. In people of Afro-Caribbean and Mediterranean origin sickle cell disease and other haemoglobinopathies are also major risk factors for stroke.

Hypertension
There is no agreement on the optimal time to start antihypertensive medication after stroke in patients who present with a raised BP, but have no previous history of hypertension. A cautious approach to treatment in these patients is justified, as a rise in BP may be a transient and direct effect of stroke. Furthermore, reduction of BP in the early post-stroke phase may conceivably increase the infarct size by reducing the regional cerebral blood flow which further compromises the metabolism in the ischaemic penumbra (see chapter 2). This is probably more important in older patients who usually need a comparatively higher BP than young patients to maintain adequate cerebral blood flow because of arteriosclerosis. Consequently, it is reasonable to delay the initiation of antihypertensive treatment in this group of patients until after the first week of stroke. However, patients with severe hypertension on presentation and those with clinical evidence of

long-standing (but previously undiagnosed) hypertension should be treated without delay. These are patients with hypertensive retinopathy and/ or with electrocardiographic or radiological evidence of left ventricular hypertrophy (in the absence of other causes such as aortic stenosis). Generally, patients with a past history of hypertension should continue to take their prescribed antihypertensive drugs without interruption even in the first week of stroke, unless their BP is too low.

Reduction of blood pressure to the target values shown in table 6.1 cuts the risk of stroke by 40% over a period of 5 years. It is important to emphasise that the benefit of treatment is usually greatest in those with the highest risk. The BP in this subgroup of patients should be monitored carefully and patients in whom optimal BP control is not achieved quickly should be referred to a specialist hypertension clinic.

A modest reduction in BP is possible with measures that include reduction of the dietary salt intake and body weight, and increase in physical activity. However, drug treatment remains the mainstay of management of hypertension and better and more sustained BP control is often achieved only when drug treatment is combined with the appropriate changes in lifestyle. In most patients a thiazide diuretic, β blocker or a calcium antagonist is a good first line treatment. If a β-blocker is contra indicated or ineffective and in patients with heart failure the use of an angiotensin-converting enzyme (ACE) inhibitor is a good option. It is advisable to avoid β blockers for the control of BP in hypertensive diabetic patients, as these drugs may induce insulin resistance. Another disadvantage of β-blocker is that they tend to mask the clinical manifestations of hypoglycaemia. Nonetheless, the use of β blockers may be justified in diabetic patients with a history of myocardial infarction because of their cardioprotective effect.

Hypertension and diabetes mellitus frequently occur together. Loop diuretics (e.g. furosemide, bumetanide) are a good alternative to thiazides in diabetic patients and in those with renal impairment. They do not interfere with glucose metabolism and they are also more effective in patients with impaired renal function. It is recommended that the blood pressure-lowering drug regimen for diabetic patients should also include an ACE inhibitor because these drugs also reduce nephropathy and proteinuria.

Table 6.1 – drug therapy of hypertension in stroke patients

Population	When to treat	Target BP	First choice drug
Age <65	≥140/90	130/85	Thiazide diuretic, β blocker
Age >65	≥160/95 or SBP ≥160	140/90	Thiazide diuretic, Ca^{+2} channel blocker
Type I diabetes	≥130/85	≤120/80	ACE inhibitor
Type II diabetes	≥130/85	≤120/80	low dose non-thiazide diuretic
Diabetic ne-phropathy	≥130/85	≤120/80	ACE inhibi-tors
Afro-Caribbeans	≥140/90	≤130/85	Diuretic, Ca^{+2} channel blocker

ACE inhibitors also appear to reduce the risk of stroke recurrence by a mechanism that is independent of their BP lowering effect. These drugs have been shown to reduce the inflammatory response and to stabilise the atherosclerotic plaque in experimental animal models. They are now recommended in the treatment of all diabetics, irrespective of their BP levels, unless when there is a clear contra-indication to their use. ACE inhibitors are contra-indicated if the serum creatinine is >200 μmol/ l, and in patients with renal artery stenosis.

So far, two of the ACE inhibitors, perindopril and ramipril, have been shown to reduce stroke recurrence and the incidence of myocardial infarction and cardiovascular death in patients with or without a previous history of hypertension. These drugs have a long half-life and are suitable as a once daily treatment. The average daily dose of perindopril is 4 mg and a better anti-hypertensive effect is usually obtained when it is combined with 2.5 mg of indapamide. In contrast to captopril and enalapril, perindopril is less likely to cause first dose hypotention. It also reduces BP by up to 8% in patients with moderate or severe internal carotid artery stenosis without a corresponding reduction in the overall or regional cerebral blood flow. Ramipril in a dose of 10 mg/ day is also as effective as perindopril in preventing stroke recurrence.

Diabetes mellitus
Tight glycaemic control (target glycated haemoglobin HbA1$_c$ ≤6.5%) has been shown to reduce the incidence and severity of the diabetic microvascular complications. It probably also has a favourable effect on the progression of atherosclerosis and the macrovascular complications that are associated with it. Good long-term control of hyperglycaemia is, therefore, an important aspect of the secondary stroke prevention. Patients with type 2 diabetes (who make approximately 80% of all diabetics) often require treatment with an oral hypoglycaemic agent, in addition to the standard dietary management and weight control. When treatment with the conventional oral hypoglycaemic drugs is either ineffective or is poorly tolerated insulin therapy or one of the glitazone drugs, e.g. rosiglitazone or pioglitazone, may be used in combination with metformin or a sulphonylurea. These drugs, which act by reducing insulin resistance, may also be used as an alternative to insulin.

Atrial fibrillation
Atrial fibrillation (AF) is the commonest cardiac arrhythmia and is a major risk factor for stroke and stroke recurrence. However, the magnitude of the risk in patients with non-valvular AF depends on the presence or absence of certain co-morbid conditions. Anticoagulation with warfarin is superior to treatment with antithrombotic agents, such as aspirin, in the secondary prevention of stroke in patients with AF. However, because of the potentially serious complications of warfarin theray it is important to offer this treatment only to those with a high risk for the thromboembolic complications associated with AF. Different criteria are used for the stratification of patients with AF into a high and low risk groups for stroke recurrence. Those with a previous stroke or TIA and, in addition, are hypertensive and diabetic have a high risk and should be considered for anticoagulation. Left ventricular dysfunction or heart failure in the preceding three months and old age (defined here as age over 75 years) are additional criteria used in some risk stratification schemes.

Long term anticoagulation is indicated for secondary stroke prevention in all patients with prosthetic heart valve replacement unless it is absolutely contra-indicated. Warfarin should also be prescribed for patients with non-valvular AF who fall in the high-risk group described above.

In patients with non-valvular AF the dose of warfarin should be adjusted to maintain an international normalised ratio (INR) between 2 and 3. A target INR of 2.5 for young subjects and of 2.0 for those who are 75 years of age or older probably gives the best benefit/risk ratio. The optimal time to commence anticoagulation after stroke is not known. The consensus opinion is that anticoagulation should be started 2 weeks after the cerebro-vascular event. Stroke patients appear to have an increased risk of serious haemorrhagic complications in the first 2 weeks and secondary prophylaxis, e.g. with heparin, during this period should be avoided. Studies have shown that patients who receive anticoagulation with heparin in the first 14 days have a reduced risk of stroke recurrence (and deep vein thrombosis of the lower limbs) but this benefit is offset by an increased risk of intracerebral haemorrhage. The target INR for patients with prosethetic heart valve replacement is 3-4.

The incidence of severe haemorrhage in patients with AF treated with warfarin that was reported in clinical trials is less than 3% per year. However, this may not reflect the true risk of this complication in routine clinical practice. The low incidence of severe haemorrhage in clinical trials is probably due to a combination of careful selection of patients entered into these studies, good compliance with therapy and rigorous monitoring of anticoagulation. It has been suggested that the true incidence of the haemorrhagic complications due to warfarin therapy in routine clinical practice is twice that reported in clinical trials. Predictors of an increased risk of haemorrhage are: age more than 65 years, past history of gastrointestinal bleeding, previous stroke, recent myocardial infarction, renal failure, severe anaemia and diabetes mellitus.

The risk of stroke in young patients (defined here arbitrarily as those who are <65 years old) with lone AF, i.e. AF in the absence of other disease, is relatively small. The incidence is about 1 per cent per year and the mean duration from the diagnosis of AF to an arterial thrombo-embolic event is more than 12 years. Consequently, the risk of long term anticoagulation probably outweighs the benefits in young patients with lone AF. Aspirin is, therefore, the drug of first choice for the secondary prevention of stroke in these patients.

Hyperlipidaemia

Drug treatment of hyperlipidaemia partially reverses established atherosclerosis and is an essential component of the overall strategy for the secondary prevention of coronary artery disease and stroke. Treatment for 5 years reduces the risk of stroke by a quarter irrespective of whether the patient has clinical evidence of coronary heart disease or not.

The statins (simvastatin, lovastatin atorvastatin, pravastatin and fluvastatin) inhibit cholesterol synthesis and are the drugs of first choice for the treatment of hypercholestrolaemia. By contrast, fibrates, such as bezafibrate and ciprofibrate, are more effective than statins in reducing high serum triglycerides. The current guidelines recommend that treatment should aim to reduce the total serum cholesterol levels to less than 5 mmol/l, or by 25% of the baseline value or to reduce low density lipoprotein cholesterol below 2.6 mmol/l or by 30%, whichever results in the lower concentration.

Statins are given as a single dose in the evening. Simvastatin in a start dose of 10-20 mg is the preferred first choice. The lipid lowering effect of statins is usually seen after the first four weeks of treatment. If necessary the dose is titrated up every 4-6 weeks until the target cholesterol levels are achieved. Statin treatment is most effective when it is combined with lifestyle modification, treatment of other stroke risk factors and with the use of antithrombotic medication. Once the hyperlipidaemia has been corrected it is usually sufficient to monitor the cholesterol levels only once a year.

Statins are tolerated well by most patients. The commonest unwanted effects of statins are gastrointestinal symptoms and headaches. Central nervous system (CNS) adverse effects, e.g. insomnia and paraesthesia, may also occur. Pravastatin 40 mg/ day is the least likely statin to cause CNS adverse effects because it crosses the blood-brain barrier less readily than other statins. Potentially serious adverse effects of statins are rare and include myopathy and liver dysfunction. Treatment should be discontinued if these complications occur. It is recommended that liver function tests are checked before the start of statin therapy and 3, 6 and 12 months thereafter. There is usually no need to continue monitoring liver function after the first year of treatment. The risk of statins-induced myopathy is increased when these drugs and fibrates are used together and in patients with muscle disease, hypothyroidism, renal impairment and alcohol abuse. It is recommended that baseline creatine phosphokinase (CPK) values are obtained before the start of treatment in these patients. Treatment should not be started if CPK levels are $\geq$ 5 times the upper limit of normal. Carbamazepine and phenytoin reduce the plasma concentrations of statins and the use of these drugs together should be avoided whenever possible.

Cigarette smoking
Cessation of cigarette smoking significantly reduces the risk of vascular events and this benefit is usually apparent within a few months. Unfortunately, however, most patients find it difficult to stop smoking or to abstain from it for long periods of time. This is largely due to the symptoms of nicotine withdrawal which include craving for cigarettes, hunger, weight gain, depression, insomnia, irritability and poor mental concentration. Peer pressure is also an obstacle to stopping smoking for some individuals. Nonetheless, smoking cessation programmes that combine counselling with the use of nicotine substitutes or bupropion are often effective, especially if the individual is highly motivated to give up smoking.

Nicotine replacement therapy (NRT) may be offered in the form of nicotine chewing gum, transdermal patches, sublingual tablets, nasal spray or inhalation. Treatment is usually required for three months and all nicotine formulations appear to have the same effectiveness. Unwanted effects of treatment include dizziness, nausea, headaches and palpitations. Transdermal patches may also cause skin irritation. NRT is contraindicated in the first month after stroke or TIA.

Bupropion is effective when given in a dose of 150 mg twice daily for 7-9 weeks. Nicotine withdrawal symptoms are less severe if treatment is started a week before the intended day of abstinence from smoking. The most frequently reported adverse effects of treatment are insomnia and dry mouth. Bupropion is contraindicated during pregnancy and in patients with epilepsy or bipolar depression. It should also be avoided in those with a reduced seizure threshold, such as patients with previous traumatic brain injury or alcoholics.

Lifestyle modification

It is assumed that lifestyle modification improves general health and contributes to the secondary prevention of stroke but the latter has not been confirmed in randomised controlled trials. Nonetheless, overweight patients should be advised to reduce their body weight to a Body Mass Index of between 18.5 and 25 kg/m² through a combination of reducing their daily calorie intake and regular physical exercise. The optimal amount of physical exercise varies from one person to another but 30 minutes of moderate physical activity, e.g. brisk walking, at least 5 days a week is usually sufficient.

Patients should be encouraged to eat a low fat, low salt diet and plenty of fruits and vegetables. A low fat, low salt diet is a diet where the fat content constitutes <30% of the total daily energy requirements with 7% or less saturated fat and a salt content of no more than 6g/day. The daily cholesterol intake should be reduced to 100 mg. This means that food which is rich in cholesterol, e.g. eggs, should be avoided. (The yolk of one average sized egg contains 250 mg of cholesterol). It is also recommended that the diet should contain at least 5 portions of fruit and vegetables per day and 2 portions of fish per week.

Sickle cell disease

Sickle cell disease (SCD) is an autosomal recessive disorder of haemoglobin synthesis. Homozygotes for the sickle cell gene synthesise predominantly haemoglobin S (HbS) and foetal haemoglobin (HbF). HbS is less soluble than HbA and when it releases oxygen the red blood cells deform and assume a sickle shape. Sickle cells tend to adhere to the vascular wall leading to recurrent vascular occlusion. The disease is characterised mainly by a severe haemolytic anaemia (due to the reduced life span of erythrocytes) and tissue infarctions that can occur virtually in any organ, including the central nervous system.

The management of the acute phase of stroke due to SCD should preferably be made in consultation with a specialist haematology unit. Therapeutic measures to ensure rehydration, adequate pain relief, correction of hypoxia and acidosis must be started immediately. In most cases exchange transfusion to achieve Hb concentration of 11 g/dl and to reduce HbS levels to <30% is also indicated. The use of anti-sickling drugs, such as hydroxyuria, may also be considered.

Regular top-up blood transfusions to maintain Hb concentrations at around 11 g/dl and to lower HbS to <30% appear to afford protection against stroke in children with SCD. This is true for both the primary and secondary prevention of cerebral ischaemic events. Interestingly, those with abnormal cerebral blood flow (demonstrated by transcranial Doppler ultrasound scans) seem to benefit most from transfusions. However, the age at which it is safe to stop the transfusion regime is not clear. Consequently, decisions to continue with this therapy should be weighed against the potential complications of repeated blood transfusions.

Antithrombotic therapy
Abnormalities of platelet function occur frequently in patients with diabetes mellitus and hyperlipidaemia. These abnormalities play an important role in the pathogenesis of atherosclerosis. Increased platelet activity results in proliferation of vascular smooth muscle cells and also predisposes to intra-arterial thrombus formation. Even in the absence of diabetes mellitus platelet activation is persistently enhanced in the acute and chronic phases of stroke. This provides the rationale for antiplatelet therapy for the secondary prevention of stroke. Aspirin, dipyridamole and clopidogrel are the main antiplatelet drugs in current use.

All patients presenting with an ischaemic stroke or TIA should receive an antiplatelet drug indefinitely even after all the modifiable stroke risk factors have been corrected. Aspirin appears to be as effective as warfarin for the secondary prevention of stroke in patients who do not have atrial fibrillation. It also has a better safety profile than warfarin, especially in elderly subjects, and does not require rigorous monitoring. It is generally accepted that aspirin should be prescribed for all patients with an ischaemic stroke except those with atrial fibrillation and a high thromboembolic risk in whom warfarin is the drug of first choice (see the section on atrial fibrillation). Treatment with aspirin is normally started in the first 48 hours after stroke. Clopidogrel is a suitable alternative in those who are allergic to aspirin or are unable to tolerate it.

A proportion of patients on long-term treatment with aspirin develop a further ischaemic stroke. In these patients combination therapy with aspirin 25 mg and dipyridamole MR 200 mg given twice daily should be considered. The combined protective effect of these drugs has been shown to be significantly greater than the effect of either drug alone. When compared with placebo treatment this combination prevents stroke recurrence in 58 patients of every 1000 patients treated for two years. By contrast, aspirin alone or dipyridamole alone prevent 29 and 26 events, respectively.

Aspirin inhibits platelet function by interfering with the metabolism of arachidonic acid and the synthesis of prostaglandins and thromboxane (which promote platelet aggregation). Full inhibition of platelet activity can be achieved with an aspirin dose as little as 50 mg/day. Although higher doses may not have additional therapeutic benefit, there is still some controversy regarding the optimal dose of aspirin for the prevention of ischaemic stroke. Currently most practitioners recommend an initial dose of 300 mg/ day with a maintenance dose of 75 mg daily after the first 2 weeks of treatment. Most of the adverse effects of aspirin are dose-dependent. Bleeding is the commonest adverse event of treatment with aspirin and the risk of this complication usually persists throughout the duration of exposure to the drug.

Dipyridamole MR is an effective antithrombotic agent. It inhibits platelets' aggregation and adhesion, and shortens their life span. It is used, with or without aspirin, in a dose of 200 mg twice daily. It has few adverse effects (see table 6.2) which usually occur at the start of treatment. Their incidence usually diminishes as treatment is continued.

Clopidogrel inhibits platelet aggregation by irreversibly blocking fibrinogen binding to platelet receptors. It also reduces platelets' adhesion to the vascular endothelium and prevents thrombus formation. The antiplatelet effect of clopidogrel is evident within 24 hours and it persists for more than 5 days after discontinuation of treatment.

In a dose of 75 mg/ day clopidogrel is more effective than low-dose aspirin in preventing myocardial infarction and stroke. (Major studies have shown that clopidogrel prevents 24 major vascular events per 1000 patients per year, compared to 19 events prevented by aspirin). However, the overall effect of both drugs on death due to a vascular event is similar. Furthermore, the cost of treatment with clopidogrel is substantially more than that of aspirin and the routine use of clopidogrel is difficult to justify on the basis of the cost/benefit ratio. There are, however, some exceptions. For example, it has been reported that aspirin is less effective in preventing vascular occlusion in the lower limbs than in other vascular beds. Consequently, clopidogrel is probably a better choice than aspirin and dipyridamole in stroke patients with peripheral vascular disease. It is possible that the combined use of aspirin and clopidogrel may confer a significant additional therapeutic advantage in stroke patients, but this has yet to be proved conclusively.

Table 6.2 – Dosage and adverse effects of the main antiplatelet agents

Drug	Maintenance dose	Common adverse events
Aspirin	75 mg/day	Dyspepsia, bleeding
Dipyridamole MR	200 mg b.d.	Headaches, diarrhoea
Clopidogrel	75 mg/day	Dyspepsia, diarrhoea, bleeding, skin rash

Carotid endarterectomy
Stenosis of the extracranial portion of the internal carotid artery (ICA) is an important and potentially treatable risk factor for ischaemic stroke, TIA and retinal infarction. Its presence or absence should be confirmed in all patients with an anterior circulation ischaemic stroke or TIA unless there there are contra indications for surgical treatment.

There are no reliable clinical signs of ICA stenosis. A carotid bruit is audible on auscultation in about one third of patients with moderately severe or severe stenosis. On the other hand, a carotid bruit may be present in a significant number of subjects with a normal ICA diameter. ICA stenosis is detected with radiological tests. All patients with an ischaemic stroke or TIA in the carotid artery territory who are considered possible candidates for carotid endarterctomy should be investigated for ICA stenosis. The investigation of first choice for initial screening is duplex ultrasonography which combines Doppler measurements of the blood flow velocity with visualisation of the lumen of the carotid arteries. If the carotid Doppler ultrasound scan is inconclusive, then MRI angiography is a good alternative. Intra-arterial angiography is indicated only if surgical treatment of ICA stenosis is being considered as this investigation carries a risk of stroke in approximately 1% of cases. Carotid endarterectomy (CE) is the treatment of choice of ICA stenosis, but carotid angioplasty may also be considered in some cases.

As mentioned in chapter 2, CE is indicated as an emergency procedure in cases of crescendo TIAs, acute carotid artery occlusion and stroke-in-evolution. Elective surgery should be considered in patients with a recent ischaemic stroke or TIA who have severe ipsilateral internal carotid artery stenosis (70% or more). CE within 3 months of the cerebral infarct was found to reduce the risk of a further stroke in the first year to 9% compared to 26% recurrence rate in patients who received the standard medical treatment.

The optimal timing of CE in patients with a completed stroke has not been established but is probably 4-6 weeks after the cerebral infarct in most cases. Although this delay exposes the patient to the risk of a further stroke, it is justifiable because of the high mortality of early surgery. In addition to the increased mortality, early CE may also be complicated by intracerebral haemorrhage or extension of the infarct. However, early CE may be beneficial in a small group of carefully selected patients. These are patients with a non-middle cerebral artery occlusion, a normal CT scan, normal level of consciousness and non-progressive deficit after the initial insult. CE also results in modest benefits in patients with severe but asymptomatic ICA stenosis and in those with moderately severe, i.e. 50-69%, symptomatic stenosis. CE may be offered up to 12 months after the index stroke. It is not indicated in patients with complete arterial occlusion or in patients with severe residual functional disability. The overall perioperative mortality of CE is <2% in surgical units that perform this procedure frequently. The main long-term complication of CE is restenosis, but this is uncommon and has an annual incidence rate of 1% after the first year.

Carotid angioplasty, with or without stent implantation, is used less frequently. It has a reported success rate of 80%, but restenosis may occur a few months later. It can also result in other complications, such as distal embolisation and rupture or dissection of the blood vessel. The long-term benefits of this procedure have not been fully evaluated and at present carotid angioplasty is mainly considered in patients with fibromuscular dysplasia, stenosis due to radiation and re-stenosis after CE.

RECOMMENDED FURTHER READING

Stroke risk factors
Tuszynski MH, Petito CK, Levy DE. Risk factors and clinical manifestations of pathologically verified lacunar infarctions. *Stroke* 1989; **20**: 990-999

Collins R, Peto R, MacMahon S et al. Blood pressure, stroke, and coronary heart disease. Part 2, short-term reductions in blood pressure: overview of randomised drug trials in their epidemiological context. *Lancet* 1990; **335**: 827-838

Palatini P, Mormino P, Santonastasa M, et al. Target-organ damage in stage I hypertensive subjects with white coat and sustained hypertension. Results from the HARVEST study. *Hypertension* 1998; **31**: 57-63

Staessen JA, Wang JG, Thijs L, Fagard R. Overview of the outcome trials in older patients with isolated systolic hypertension. *Journal of Human Hypertension* 1999; **13**: 859-863

PROGRESS Collaborative Group. Randomised trial of a perindopril-based blood-pressure-lowering regimen among 6105 individuals with previous stroke or transient ischaemic attack. *Lancet* 2001; **358**: 1033-1041

Bosch J, Yusuf S, Pogue J, et al. Use of ramipril in preventing stroke: double blind randomised trial. *British Medical Journal* 2002, **324**: 1-5

Beckman JA, Creager MA, Libby P. Diabetes and atherosclerosis: epidemiology, pathophysiology and management. *Journal of the American Medical Association* 2002; **287**: 2570-2581

Hart RG, Halperin JL. Atrial fibrillation and stroke. Concepts and controversies. *Stroke* 2001; **32**: 803-808

Pearce LA, Hart RG, Halperin JL. Assessment of three schemes for stratifying stroke risk in patients with non-valvular atrial fibrillation. *American Journal of Medicine* 2000; **109**: 45-51

EAFT (European Atrial Fibrillation Trial) Study Group. Secondary prevention in non-rheumatic atrial fibrillation after transient ischaemic attack and minor stroke. *Lancet* 1993; **342**: 1255-1262

Kopecky SL, Gersh BJ, McGoon MD, et al. The natural history of lone atrial fibrillation. *New England Journal of Medicine* 1987; **316**: 669-674.

The Stroke Prevention in Atrial Fibrillation Investigators. Predictors of thrombo-embolism in atrial fibrillation. Clinical features of patients at risk. *Annals of Internal Medicine* 1992; **116**: 1-5.

Hebert PR, Gaziano JM, Chan KS, Hennekens CH. Cholesterol lowering with statin drugs, risk of stroke, and total mortality. An overview of randomized trials. *Journal of the American Medical Association* 1997; **278**: 313-321

Howard G, Wagenknecht LE, Burke GL, et al. Cigarette smoking and progression of atherosclerosis: the Atherosclerosis Risk in Communities (ARIC) Study. *Journal of the American Medical Association* 1998; **279**: 119-124

Ohene-Frempong K, Weiner SJ, Sleeper LA, et al. Cooperative study of sickle cell disease. Cerebrovascular accidents in sickle cell disease: rates and risk factors. *Blood* 1998; **91**: 288-294

Adams RJ, McKie VC, Hsu L, et al. Prevention of a first stroke by transfusions in children with sickle cell anemia and abnormal results on transcranial Doppler ultrasonography. *New England Journal of Medicine* 1998; **339**: 5-11

Antithrombotic therapy

Laguna P, Martin A, Del Arco C, et al. Differences among clinical classification schemes for predicting stroke in atrial fibrillation: implications for therapy in daily practice. *Academic Emergency Medicine* 2005; **12**: 828-834

Van Kooten F, Ciabattoni G, Koudstaal PJ, et al. Increased platelet activation in the chronic phase after cerebral ischaemia and intracerebral haemorrhage. *Stroke* 1999; **30**: 546-549

Smith NM, Pathansali R, Bath PM. Platelets and stroke. *Vascular Medicine* 1999; **4**: 165-172

International Stroke Trial Collaborative Group. The international stroke trial (IST): a randomised trial of aspirin, subcutaneous heparin, both or neither among 19,435 patients with acute ischaemic stroke. *Lancet* 1997; **349**: 1569-81.

Mohr JP, Thompson JLP, Lazar RM, et al. A comparison of warfarin and aspirin for the prevention of recurrent ischaemic stroke. *New England Journal of Medicine* 2001; **345**: 1444-1451

CAPRIE Steering Committee. A randomised, blinded, trial of clopidogrel versus aspirin in patients at risk of ischaemic events (CAPRIE). *Lancet* 1996; **348**: 1329-1339

Diener H, Cunha L, Forbes C, et al. European stroke prevention study 2. Dipyridamole and acetylsalicylic acid in the secondary prevention of stroke. *Journal of the Neurological Sciences* 1996; **143**: 1-13

Carotid endarterectomy

North American Symptomatic Carotid Endarterectomy Trial Collaborators. Beneficial effect of carotid endarterectomy in symptomatic patients with high-grade carotid stenosis. *New England Journal of Medicine* 1991; **325**: 445-453

Executive Committee for the Asymptomatic Carotid Atherosclerosis Study. Endarterectomy for asymptomatic carotid artery stenosis. *Journal of the American Medical Association* 1996; **273**: 1421-1428

Hsia DE, Moscoe LM, Krushat WM. Epidemiology of carotid endarterectomy among Medicare beneficiaries. *Stroke* 1998; **29**: 346-350

Index

60, 61, 63, 71, 77, 80, 86, 87,
88, 95, 106, 112, 113, 116, 142,
153, 169, 170

C

Carotid artery stenosis 7, 10, 16, 29,
164, 167, 175, 178
Caudate nucleus, stroke involving 17,
18, 21, 64
Cigarette smoking 7, 9, 10, 22, 34,
105, 164, 170, 177
Clopidogrel – see antithrombotic
drugs 51, 172, 173, 174, 177
Cognitive impairment 22, 25, 32, 46,
78, 94, 95, 103, 105, 106, 110,
117, 125, 156

D

Depression, after stroke 15, 27, 31,
32, 38, 39, 40, 44, 46, 49, 51,
53, 60, 63, 71, 73, 79, 85, 86,
87, 88, 89, 92, 93, 94, 96, 101,
106, 108, 109, 110, 112, 120,
122, 123, 124, 125, 132, 139,
140, 141, 142, 147, 148, 151,
156, 157, 159, 160, 161, 164,
168, 170, 172
Diaschisis 18, 38, 40, 41, 54
Dipyridamole – see antithrombotic
drugs 51, 172, 173, 174, 177
Discharge from hospital 147, 149,
151, 152, 153, 156
Driving, after stroke 15, 27, 31, 32,
38, 39, 40, 44, 46, 49, 51, 53,
71, 73, 79, 85, 86, 87, 88, 89,
92, 93, 94, 96, 101, 108, 109,
110, 112, 120, 122, 123, 124,
139, 140, 141, 142, 147, 148,
151, 156, 157, 158, 159, 160,
161, 164, 168, 170, 172
Dysarthria 21, 23, 25, 60, 70, 71, 88,
103, 148
Dysarthria-clumsy hand syndrome 23
Dysphagia – assessment 7, 15, 21, 25,

44, 47, 48, 60, 61, 66, 67, 68,
71, 72, 74, 75, 79, 83, 87, 88,
89, 90, 97, 98, 99, 103, 112,
113, 114, 115, 116, 117, 118,
119, 120, 121, 122, 130, 142,
146, 147, 148, 151, 152, 156,
157, 159, 164, 176
clinical manifestations 8, 12, 25, 35,
113, 131, 165, 176
complications of 8, 43, 50, 116, 131,
154, 167, 172
dietary modification 44, 48, 118
differential diagnosis 23, 66, 67, 82,
95, 97, 102, 115
management 1, 7, 12, 13, 16, 25,
34, 44, 45, 50, 52, 53, 57, 61,
88, 90, 91, 92, 93, 95, 101, 102,
104, 106, 107, 113, 116, 118,
130, 131, 138, 139, 143, 146,
148, 149, 153, 155, 160, 164,
165, 167, 171, 176
Dysphasia – assessment 18, 20, 21,
25, 60, 61, 62, 63, 64, 65, 66,
67, 68, 69, 70, 72, 74, 75, 94,
103, 148, 156
Broca's 41, 61, 63, 64, 65, 70, 73
classification 12, 13, 14, 35, 63, 65,
68, 177
clinical features 12, 13, 14, 16, 20,
23, 24, 33, 62, 80, 82, 123, 140,
176
differential diagnosis 23, 66, 67, 82,
95, 97, 102, 115
drug treatment 26, 44, 70, 86, 102,
124, 160, 165, 169
prognosis 1, 12, 13, 14, 16, 30, 31,
32, 34, 35, 40, 46, 51, 63, 66,
70, 86, 92, 107, 113, 149, 156,
158
Wernicke's 62, 65, 73

E

Embolism 9, 10, 11, 12, 15, 19, 20,
30, 31, 33, 46, 112, 140, 141,
176

locked in 21, 22

T

Therapy – cognitive 154
  Occupational 148, 154, 155, 157,
    158
  physical 15, 25, 38, 43, 44, 67, 79,
    91, 103, 106, 115, 129, 137,
    146, 147, 148, 152, 153, 156,
    159, 160, 161, 165, 171
  Speech and language 69, 70, 113,
    154
Thrombolysis 27, 40, 45, 48, 49, 51,
    146
Thrombophilia 30
Thrombosis - in-situ 11
  deep vein 11, 46, 112, 130, 139, 168
Todd's paralysis 24
Transient ischaemic attacks 33, 146

U

Urodynamic studies 99

V

Visual impairment 87

W

Warfarin, use in stroke prevention 51,
    141, 167, 168, 172, 176, 177

Printed in the United Kingdom
by Lightning Source UK Ltd.
123681UK00001B/276/A